Letters

from

Vietnam

By: Joseph Allen Freeborn
His Story

Outskirts Press, Inc.
http://www.outskirtspress.com

ISBN: 978-1-9772-1486-7

Library of Congress Control Number: 2019908990

Web Site: *lettersfromvietnambook.com*

Cover Design © 2019 by Bella Design Group, Lake Zurich, IL. All rights reserved - Used with permission.

Outskirts Press and the "OP" logo are trademarks belonging to Outskirts Press, Inc.

PRINTED IN THE UNITED STATES OF AMERICA

ACKNOWLEDGMENTS

Bob Hampel, my good friend and fellow Vietnam veteran. You encouraged me to keep writing and convinced me the story was worth telling. So I did.

To my loving wife Angie, who quietly and consistently supported the hours I spend researching this work and the years I struggled writing it. *Thanks for waiting.*

To my brothers of Bravo Company 1st/46th–196th Light Infantry Brigade, this is your story too. We all lived the events I talk about here. You were a brave and tough bunch of young men. I salute you all, **Welcome Home!**

Contents

Introduction–Letters from Vietnam

This story represents thousands of stories over the ten-year span of the Vietnam War. Safe or secure places in Vietnam did not exist. The enemy did not discriminate; they went after everyone, every rank and gender, military or civilian that opposed their ideology.

This book depicts a snapshot in time during a very divisive war and how it affected the author's decisions, moods and wellbeing. The letters are copies of the exact text from the mail he sent and received. There are instances names were changed, but the content of the letters are accurate. These letters were saved by the author and he carefully preserved them when he returned home. They stood as a reminder of those days in Nam. He would read some of them from time to time, trying to make sense of this senseless war. In 1985, shortly after his Dad's death, he found all the letters he had written his Dad. He cherished them all.

He was fortunate to have his job waiting for him when he returned from Nam, his girlfriend had waited for him and his friends were supportive. These things were crucial to his successful integration to civilian life, but the war continued to nag him. "Why me?" he would ponder. "Why was I the only person in my high school graduating class to be drafted and sent to Vietnam?"

These questions haunted the author for years after returning home. Troubled and confused, he sat down with his Dad one day and opened up to his feelings. Hesitant and ashamed, he told his Dad how he felt betrayed and used. He felt singled out having to risk his life, livelihood and entire future on an unjust war. His Dad, a World War II veteran and prisoner of war, listened and reflected on everything he said. He then replied, "Joey, we cannot pick the wars our country gets involved in, all we can do is respond to them. Your service to the country was needed, and you stepped up. You proved to yourself what you were made of, and you proved to your country, you are a patriot."

The author had been steeped in self-pity and shame, the America he returned to influenced those feelings. That day was the beginning of his healing, which continues to this day.

He served, survived and wrote this book for future generations to better understand the effects of the Vietnam War.

Chapter 1

It was hot! About 95 degrees as close as I could figure; the day was dry and clear, blue skies, with a few high puffy white clouds, not the way I imagined this place to be.

Cam Rahn Bay, South Vietnam, was a small strategic seaport built and operated by the 18th Engineering Brigade. The 124th Transport Command took over this base in April 1971.

We arrived at the airfield on August 3, 1971, around 10 AM. I expected to have to get off the plane shooting. As I came to the doorway, I saw the bright sun-filled day; and was intently listening for automatic weapon fire, but heard none. As I came down the stairs and walked into the warm sunlight, I remember thinking what a strange place.

The terrain was mountainous around the north and east boundaries. I could see the South China Sea as I walked towards the small terminal. I noticed sand everywhere; it looked hot and loose, nothing growing on it, like a beach, with buildings all around. Once through the terminal, I realized how hot and loose the sand was; my brand-new jungle boots sank into the sand nearly to my ankles, making walking difficult. I could feel the heat of the sand through my boots, everything here was hot! I started to become annoyed after only a few minutes in country.

We assembled in front of the small hut to get our assignments for work details, bunks, mess information, etc. I remember seeing four GIs across a small roadway waiting for the next "Freedom Bird" back to the world. They had blank hardened looks on their faces and appeared to be in a trance. They were haggard and tired looking, their clothes were shabby, and they weren't Army issue. I remember thinking it would take me 12 months (my full tour of duty) to get from here to there, assuming I made it out of here at all.

What the hell was I doing here? I disliked this place; that smelly smoke off at a distance was making me nauseous. Beads of sweat formed as I stood waiting in the sweltering heat. It was like a bad dream.

Later that morning, a few of us newbies were sitting around a table in the EM club. We were uncomfortably hot, despite the few slowly rotating fans blowing the warm air around. We sat there trying to enjoy a cheeseburger of sorts, not very authentic, but after all this was Nam. Except for a few new arrivals, the club was empty. The heat was too much for the regular permanent party personnel (military personnel permanently stationed there); they knew where the cool places were. We sat there for a time sweating, discussing this strange place. The fear we all felt was thinly masked, I kept thinking just 24 hours ago I was in Seattle, Washington. Now I stood at the gates of hell.

I found my first letter to Dad difficult to write; it took a few days to collect my thoughts and get them on paper. I'm sure he was eager to hear from me.

I recall leaving my Dad standing at the end of the sidewalk; I had this image burned in my memory. We walked out of the house; I was a few steps ahead of him carrying my duffel bag. When I got to the end of the sidewalk, I stopped and waited a second for him to reach me. I glanced at him and he turned away, not wanting to face this goodbye, or me. The look on his face was flush as to cry. He wouldn't cry however, as I only saw him cry twice, once when his mother died and once when my mother died. His pride would not allow any signs of weakness now; his little boy was going to war, he needed to be strong for both of us. I extended my hand to shake his; he grabbed me and said "good luck." I mumbled something like take care of yourself; the exchange was awkward, neither of us wanted to say goodbye. I knew how proud he was of me, I knew he loved me; I knew he would worry about me every day and pray for me. I turned and shoved my bag into the trunk of Angie's car. As we drove off, I looked back to see my Dad standing at the end of the sidewalk.

My girlfriend Angie was kind enough to take me to the bus station that morning. We tried to keep the conversation light when we spoke. The 20-minute ride to the bus station was uncomfortable for both of us, we had so much to say, but words were hard coming. In training they told us to forget your girlfriends at home. They would not be waiting for you, I didn't dwell on this but I knew it was a real possibility. I wasn't even sure if I was coming home. I had a one-way ticket, with an uncertain future. Unfortunately Angie had feelings for the guy who drew the short straw and was heading out to that despicable place. I was lucky she was giving me a lift; let alone her waiting for me.

When we got to the bus station in Newburgh, I didn't prolong the goodbye. I told her again I loved her and would write soon, and she affirmed her love for me and would also write. It was difficult for both of us. I

4

promised I'd be careful and told her I'd miss her. We kissed and then I boarded the bus to JFK Airport.

On the evening of my first day at Cam Rahn Bay, I was scared and homesick. I was in the tightest jam of my 20 years, green and scared of the unknown horrors this place might have in store. My stomach was upset, I was thirsty and the nearest latrine (bathroom) was somewhere across the dark sandy compound. I didn't know where anything was; I resigned myself to snooping around the next day to get the lay of the land. Thirsty, sweaty and exhausted, I drifted off to sleep, thinking tomorrow might be better.

The next three days weren't much better; I woke the first morning to that sickening odor, the smell I had encountered yesterday. The hazy black smoke seemed to envelop my small cramped quarters. What the hell was that raunchy smell? I'd find out later; now I needed a shower and a latrine. I gathered up my stuff and set out to locate the latrine.

They told me they're burning shit. They did this to keep the base sanitary as there was no sewer system at the camp. Drain waste water would run down small trenches dug in the sand. The solid waste and urine was collected and burnt.

Around the base were wooden huts with 4 to 6 holes cut out in the bench seats. I knew these huts as outhouses; in Nam they were called 'shitters'. Under these huts were compartments that held 55-gallon drums, cut in half. When the drums got full, a lucky 'volunteer' (usually assigned as disciplinary action) would drag these drums out, douse them with 5 gallons of diesel fuel and set them on fire. The smell was awful causing me to gag and become nauseous. This encounter with burning feces combined with kerosene, lingered in my memory of smells for years. For me it was the stink that defined Vietnam.

August 4, 1971, I checked in with the Company Clerk for my work assignment. He told me I had "garbage detail today, report to Sgt. Woods at the mess hall, he'll fill you in."

"Get up on that deuce and a half, we're goin' for a ride," Woods instructed.

"Where?" I nervously questioned.

"Never mind, you'll see," was his reply.

I jumped onto the truck loaded with barrels of garbage, cardboard boxes and various junk. I guess we're going to the dump. My guess was confirmed as we pulled into the largest open landfill I had ever seen. Nothing but piled up garbage.

The countryside just outside Cam Rahn Bay appeared tranquil. Rolling hills of green reed grass, small villages, people doing their business, no one was shooting at us, and we were not shooting at anyone. This place seemed surreal. The 3 mile trip to the dump was pleasant, except for the rotting stench of garbage. Abruptly the picture changed as we pulled into this large hole filled with garbage.

I observed something unusual; older men, women, and children wandering around the dumpsite. As the truck got in position to off load the garbage, the people began to walk towards our truck. As they approached, the Sgt. shouted at them in Vietnamese, tro lai, tro lai, in other words stay away. He kept yelling at them, but they ignored his command and began climbing onto the truck. Sgt. Woods ordered me to dump the barrels as he pushed the people off the truck. They kept climbing on, only to be pushed off again. I got the barrels emptied, and the driver pulled away. I watched these people going through the rotting garbage and collecting scraps.

August 7, 1971

Dear Dad,

How are you? I'm sorry for the delay in writing, but with the heat and adjusting to this place, I couldn't seem to sit down and write.

I arrived in Vietnam August 3, 1971 to a place called Cam Rahn Bay. A replacement station located on the south central coastline. I was there for 3 days, and was then sent to Chu Lai, located about 200 miles north of Cam Rahn Bay. I am in Chu Lai now, and will be for about 6 days. They have a six-day classroom session, which will consist of a review of everything that has been taught to us for the last 4 months.

I just completed processing my financial records. I had a $100 allotment taken out; it will be sent to you each month. I also want to save $100 each month, but I'm not sure of having enough to do so. The allotment will start in September, so if I can, I will mail $75 home this month via a money order. It's not easy to do this in country.

I have been assigned to the 23rd Infantry Americal Division. Do not know where, and I won't know until I'm through in Chu Lai. I'll probably be going somewhere near Da Nang. That is quite a way north, near the DMZ. There

8

is talk of fierce action up in that area, and others report nothing is going on. I don't believe either of the stories.

It is sure hard to believe I'm in Vietnam. Life is very different in this country. The weather was a bit warmer, and water is a welcome sight. I should mention the ocean, which I can see from my bunk; it is just about the cleanest, most beautiful body of water I've ever seen. I think it's the South China Sea. We are not allowed to swim in it however due to a lack of certified lifeguards that sure is a joke! I could hump in the bush, but I can't swim in the ocean without a lifeguard.

August 8, 1971 (letter continued)

Well Dad, here I am again, I got sidetracked from this letter, but I'm determined to finish it. I just completed my first day of classes, they were pretty interesting. But as time goes on they'll probably get boring. I'm just trying to get everything out of them though.

Today being Sunday, I wanted to go to church, and I did, the only problem was the chaplain didn't show. I'm a bit disappointed; I was counting on going all week. I missed church last Sunday because I got up too late. I need to rap with a chaplain about now. I'm confused about a few things. I always heard that while in the Army, one could lose his faith in God and in his church. I met a guy who claimed he was saved. We talked at length about how he invited Jesus Christ into his heart and into his life. In order for him to do this he had to denounce all worldly pleasures, and could not attend regular church services. His idea for salvation was good, but many of his beliefs contradicted the teachings of the Catholic Church, and I felt as if his Bible was worded differently from ours. I was really bummed out; I didn't believe the impact his little sermon had on me. My head is a lot clearer now, but now especially, I feel I need to definitely shore up my faith. I have a Bible now, and I will definitely make good use of it.

I started this letter in a cheerful frame of mind even though I'm extremely unhappy here. I don't want to complain to you. It would not make me a bit happier, I do want you to know however I'm going to be straight infantry, I will not be in the rear area at all, and I'll be spending much of my tour here in the bush. I can't understand why I was chosen for this, I was hoping for a break when I got here, but now I know I was dreaming. I will do the best job I can, and my mission is to get back to the world as soon as possible.

Well, I guess I've written enough about the situation. I'll try to keep my letters on the cheerful side, this *one is not too cheerful, so don't let it bother you. I'm going to a movie tonight, and last night I saw a show at the EM club, it was very good. It's good to preoccupy yourself while in Nam; I learned that today in class. So dad, take care of yourself and give my best to the kids. I'll try to write again soon. Oh yeah, don't use the return address on this letter, it's only temporary. I'll be getting a permanent one soon. Well take care.*

Love, Joey.

My conversion in faith had started. I didn't realize it yet, but the encounter with that born again Christian in Seattle, Washington had changed me. He instilled in me a brand-new idea, an idea I could have a personal relationship with Jesus. I had learned about Jesus, but had no concept of a personal relationship with Him. This idea of a friendship with God was foreign to me, but somehow seemed possible. I prayed for the understanding and soon Jesus would reveal himself in a very personal way.

The next few days would be unsettling for me. The classroom type instructions went on for three or four days. Veterans of jungle warfare (grunts) instructed us; some with two and three tours of duty.

The wooden amphitheater type structures (classrooms) were built around the perimeter of this base camp. We sat on hard wooden benches and tried to pay attention. I remember being eager to get started with my new unit. The instructions seemed endless, but before long a group of us boarded a C-130 transport plane, heading north to the large coastal city of Da Nang.

The short flight to Da Nang took about an hour. The web seating was uncomfortable, and I found the box lunch we got before boarding interesting. I remember thinking how unusual it was to be given this small box with a few packaged items for a relatively short trip. I guess it was just something to keep us occupied.

The airport was large and sprawling, like the military air bases in the states. The Air Force had been here for a while, it was well established. There were Air Force personnel everywhere and a young, neatly dressed NCO (non-commissioned officer) met us. They called our names, and instructed us to fall in behind one of the sergeants. The sergeant I lined up behind seemed to be easy-going, not like a DI (Drill Instructor); he turned to us and said, "Welcome to the Nam." He continued telling us we would get aboard a deuce and a half for the short trip to our company area. The stop at the company area was a pleasant surprise. I expected going directly out to the

12

bush where we would be handed a weapon and the war would begin. It didn't happen that way, thank God.

The trip to Company B 1st Battalion 46th Infantry Division of the 196 Infantry Brigade was short. The roadway was two lanes, paved and well maintained. There were both civilian and military vehicles on the road and lots of pedestrian traffic. We passed one small village after another, tin covered hootches, with opened fronts and the other three sides enclosed. You could look into the dwellings and see people living in there. There were lots of children and older men and women. I was really in the Third World now I thought. The truck made a few sharp turns, slowed, then came to an abrupt stop; we were home.

The buildings were small screened-in wood structures, with doors on either end. Bunks were neatly arranged along both sides of a center aisle. No footlockers or closets, just bunks. We were told to take any one we wanted, but to fallout in 15 minutes, Top (Company's First Sergeant) wanted to see us, the Company Clerk instructed. I stood in the middle of this cramped, stuffy room, with no air moving. It was like an oven inside and I attributed that to the corrugated metal ceiling. The only sign of prior occupancy were the words "Arnold Ziffel" spray-painted on the inside metal ceiling.

Arnold Ziffel I thought, maybe that was the pig from the TV show Green Acres?

Fall in! Someone shouted, I guess that means me, 15 minutes had not passed, but I knew we were being called out. A short, tough looking Sergeant with stripes and hash marks covering his entire shirt sleeve was standing there. We quickly fell into formation; it would be one of the last formations for me in Vietnam. (Formation is one or more straight lines of soldiers standing at attention.)

"My name is First Sergeant Williams," he barked.

"Welcome to got dam Vietnam! We've been waiting on ya'all; we're short men in the bush. I don't want you to get too comfortable here as you will move out at 0800 hours tomorrow morning. You will be issued your field gear this afternoon, instructed how to pack a rucksack, and will draw your weapon and ammo at 0730 tomorrow morning, just before your chopper leaves. I will debrief you on the mission so your heads are not totally up your ass when you get out there. It's hot (being fired on) and we've been hit today. You're needed out there ASAP, so let's get going, you've got a lot to do, fall out."

HOT! I thought, what the hell was that? Because of Top's reference to being hit, the Company was under attack. How were we going to help? We were newbies, virtually useless for the first 2 to 4 weeks in the bush. This was when newbies learned survival tactics and got connected with seasoned grunts. Time was wasting and that Company Clerk was heading our way.

"Okay, you guys listen up, my name is Post, Sergeant Mike Post, you newbies can call me Mike. We will head over to S4 supply area. They will issue your web gear and I'll instruct you how to put everything together. You will turn in the clothes issued to you before you got here. These clothes will be replaced with field gear, no rank, no unit insignias, no names, nothing, the only identification will be your dog tags, any questions? Good, let's move out."

S4 supply comprised of a large metal building, filled with everything we needed. We had lots of stuff thrown at us, our sizes were guesstimated, and everything fit well enough. Our boots were the only new issue we got to keep; newbies always had black boots.

Mike went over his well-rehearsed spiel on stuffing our rucksacks, I had to empty mine and do it my way. His way wasted a lot of valuable space and just made little sense. I finally strapped on my ruck, and after a few adjustments, it felt okay. Mike told us the ruck weighed about 80 pounds; mine didn't, not yet.

The Company area was quiet, almost desolate. I threw my stuff on the end of the bunk and wondered, what the #&@# was I doing here? I was getting a real sense of the situation. I felt weak and upset, and if I didn't have to go out to the bush, my chances for survival might increase. But what would I do here, this place is boring, I'm a grunt now, I had to accept it.

They would issue my M16 weapon tomorrow morning; the ammo would be ready for us later today. We had to get our ammo loaded in magazines and then secured in bandoliers. I remembered how to do that from my AIT (Advanced Infantry Training) in Fort Polk. I wanted to get my gear together in advance as tomorrow would be too hectic. I pushed my rucksack off the end of the bed and stretched out on the bunk. I wouldn't see a bed for a while so I had better take advantage of it. A few minutes later I was asleep.

I woke up startled! How long had I been asleep? Where were the other guys? I looked at my watch; I hadn't been asleep long. I looked around and found the guys outside talking.

"Hey look its sleepy," they laughed and then continued, "yeah, I heard it was hot as hell, pinned down for days."

I interrupted, "what are you talking about?"

Jim spoke up, "Marble Mountain man, that's where we're going tomorrow."

"Who told you that?" I insisted.

"I was rapping with that Company Clerk Mike, he filled me in, man he's uptight about it too. It seems he was buddies with one guy who got killed. You know Mike was out in the bush for a few months, and he's going home soon."

Pinned down, how awful. I felt sick again, nerves, fear of the unknown. I attempted to shake off these feelings, trying to change the subject,

"Hey, have you heard when we will get our ammo issued?" I asked.

"Nope, Mike will get with us after lunch," Jim answered.

"What'd ya say we go over to the mess hall; I'm starvin'."

The uneasiness of the recent news made me queasy. I had nothing to eat since the box lunch hours ago, maybe that was my problem. Let's go we agreed and set out across the compound for the mess hall.

Sharing these tense times with these guys made things better for me. We laughed and made jokes, nervous comments, and just kept the conversation going. The mess hall was small, the food was sparse. They only had us and a few REMPS (rear echelon military personnel) to feed. I don't recall what I ate, a little of this and some of that, just enough to feel satisfied. I had my first cup of coffee of the day; it was okay, not as good as the stateside Army coffee. The mess hall had real milk, and lots of it, juices and soft drinks, bread, butter, most of the conveniences of home. Tomorrow this would all be a dream. Soon I'd be eating out of tin cans (c-rations) and freeze-dried bags (LRPPs - long range patrol packets).

We got back to the Company area to find Top (First Sergeant Williams) pacing around, apparently looking for us.

"Where the hell were you guys?" he shouted! "We need to get you squared away ASAP. I need you in the bush today. You need to get to the armory, clean your weapons, draw your ammo and get ready to go. Things have changed; the gun ships have taken out the dink stronghold, they're retreating into the bush. Captain Mac radioed, he wants you in today so the unit can move sooner. Be ready to go by 1500 hours. That's all I can tell you; your squad leader will square you away when you're out there. I have Sgt. Post waiting on you, so move out; I'll see ya back here at 1300 hours."

Oh man, the shit just hit the fan. I'm not ready for this, but ready or not.... We hurried down to the armory hootch, Mike was there waiting on us.

"Did Top see you guys?" he shouted!

"Yeah." I said.

"Let's go chop-chop, we've got a shitload to do," Mike barked back. "It's better for you guys this way; at least you won't be going into a hot LZ, that's what we're told, anyway. Hot LZs are no fun, I've been there, they suck."

We were shit'n our pants, and Mike knew it. He needed us to keep alert and focused on the situation. After about a half hour, we did almost everything. The ammo was the only thing left. They gave us a box full of loose ammo, a bag full of Army issue 20 round magazines and we had to fill as many as we could. We also drew grenades and willie pete (white phosphorus) and some colored smoke canisters. I had a lot of ammo. Now I knew why the rucks weighed 80 pounds, the ammo alone was 30 pounds. They also gave us belts of pig ammo; that is M60 machine gun ammo. Mike said, "if you want to make friends out in the bush, go out with lots of pig ammo, everyone carries it. They're low on pig ammo and need you to bring some out." I strapped it on!

I looked like Pancho Villa with this 30 caliber machine gun ammo strapped across me in an X pattern. In addition, I had my rucksack, grenades, a full week supply of rations, three days' worth of water in canteens, bedroll, poncho, poncho liner and a deflated air mattress. My bedding was rolled up under my rucksack and attached with bungee cords. I hooked at least 3 D-rings on and had M16 ammo stashed wherever. I was now feeling like a grunt, my uniform was old and faded, I had a bush hat and a steel pot, my fatigue pant legs wrapped tightly around my calves, just as the Sergeant had instructed.

"Leeches," he said, "would crawl up your legs, and find a nice warm place in your crotch if you didn't wrap your legs like this. Never walk around with your pants un-bloused."

We looked at each other and said, "let's go!" and walked the short distance to the chopper pad.

My first letter from the bush:

August 18, 1971

Dear Dad,

Hi, how's everything. I hope you received my last letter, with my new address included. I'm really looking forward to hearing from you   Well, I've been here now for two weeks and I can't believe it's only been two weeks. Time drags on, and if you're busy, you are not aware of it. My complete tour over here will be 12 months. I thought it was for 10, but I was misinformed. I'm now with a good unit, or so it seems. I'm learning a lot about Vietnam. I feel fortunate or lucky I guess.

I left Chu Lai last Saturday for Da Nang. I'm nowhere near the city of Da Nang, but it's just as well, for the city and all villages are off-limits to Army personnel. It used to be a big deal when a G. I. went to Da Nang, it was almost like the world (US), because it's a big city with many things to do, they're having trouble with "Cowboys" (Vietnamese Hippies) fighting with G. I.'s trying to kill us.

Now, I'm on my first mission as an infantry soldier. We left yesterday morning (Monday). We are located in a place called Marble Mountain, a firebase about 15 miles from Da Nang. We are on standby right now, and waiting word to go on to a village which may be hiding large amounts of rockets, etc. I imagine it will be interesting. But for now, we are just hanging around under helicopter hangers, waiting.

Well, I guess I'll end it here. I've got more to tell you but I can't think anymore now. I hope to hear from you soon, I'll try to write often. I don't know how often though. Take care of yourself, say hello to everyone for me.

Love, Joey.

Chapter 2

August 1970 I began my working life. I had just bought my dream car, a 1967 Mediterranean blue Pontiac Firebird, 4 speed, 326 V8 engine, a big step up for a guy who drove VW's and Corvairs up to this point. This car was my focal point, I would wash it almost daily, I kept the interior spotless and the gas tank full. I installed a top of the line eight-track tape player. Finally, I owned a car I could be proud of.

After high school I attended Ulster County Community College for one year. I couldn't wait to get out of school and get to work, so I could buy the things I wanted. This sense of independence always motivated me.

My first real job came in June 1970 with Taconic Data Research, a small subcontracting firm for IBM. Don Wickes, owner and manager, employed about 15 employees. He split the business into three segments; a Keypunch Department, a Technical Writing Department and a Technical Illustration Department.

I was hired as an entry-level Technical Illustrator. My background was drafting, and I had a good eye for visualization. The skills I learned in mechanical drawing helped me land this job. The process involved studying orthographic drawings (3 view drawing), then sketching the parts for visualization and orientation. I would typically have a pad full of sketches before going to the layout. I drew the layout on vellum using pencil. I would draw a fully exploded isometric, three-dimensional drawing for approval. Once approved, I proceeded to the next step.

The process of developing the exploded parts manual for IBM was very detailed. Everything had to be done to an exact standard. Lettering sizes, line widths, arrowhead sizes, etc., all had to be uniform from sheet to sheet. IBM technicians used these manuals for field repairs on the IBM Selectric typewriters. The manuals served as a reference for them when troubleshooting and ordering parts. The manuals were about 50 to 60 pages with every part exploded in the order of assembly, including a detailed parts list with quantities and part numbers. My job was to prepare the exploded views, with item numbers pointing to every part drawn. The Technical Writer prepared the parts list to complete the document.

The finished drawing was done on a 17" x 22" non-reproductive blue linen sheet. I would trace the layout in ink from the pencil layout using Rapidograph ink pens. Lettering was done using LeRoy lettering templates. This required a steady hand and an artistic eye. After completing the drawing, I applied a clear acetate overlay; applying the arrows, leader lines and balloons. These would point to the part and correspond to the parts list.

I liked what I did for a living; I had arrived, now I could plan my future.

"Don't forget Joey, I want the $25 this week; you can't expect to live here and not help out with expenses," my mother would remind me.

This reminder upset me, as I was only taking home $98 per week. I knew her reason for the request, but I resisted. The lesson was responsibility; for $25 a week I'd get my meals, a private bedroom, laundry service, and a nice home. Yet, I had trouble getting used to the idea that the free ride was over. With my mother's insistence however, I came to accept my responsibility. She never needed to remind me again.

Ruby, my mother, a small woman 5'-2", blonde hair, thin frame, never weighed over 110 pounds. Despite having a series of illnesses throughout her life, she was a strong woman. I remember how she worked full-time for Western Union in the spring, summer and early fall, and take time off during the winter months. She kept a clean, orderly home. Raising four children, she learned organization was the key to a happy home. A great cook, she enjoyed preparing meals, baking and trying to anticipate everyone's likes and needs. Eager to please, she set the tone for our home.

Her recent illness forced her to stop working; she took an extended leave of absence from the Newburgh Western Union office. She visited her doctor often, he prescribed various pain relief medications to allow her to sleep and function at some level. I noticed her health going downhill; the decline came on gradually. Her voice became weaker; she didn't have that spark in her eyes. Her illness lingering much longer than expected, with no improvement. My Dad looked into different treatments for her back pain. He contacted various doctors and hospitals over a six-month period until he found Dr. Demarest. My mother's treatment took a whole new direction under Dr. Demarest's care. He suggested surgery to find the cause of what might be a pinched nerve. They scheduled the operation for early September 1970, hoping to get Mom back on her feet.

On Tuesday, September 8, 1970 my mother checked into St. Luke's Hospital for her pre-op tests and consultation with the surgeon who would perform the delicate surgery. With the 2-day pre-op done, we couldn't wait for the operation to be over. On Thursday, September 10, they scheduled the operation. My family gathered in her room to send her off, with high hopes, we waited, and waited, and waited.

Then a man dressed in green surgical scrubs came into the waiting room and announced, "Mom is out of surgery; she's in recovery and should be back in her room within an hour."

"Mr. Freeborn," he continued, "I need to speak to you about a billing issue, follow me please."

The cancerous tumor had spread; it was not a mass, but an aggressive cancer which consumed most of her pancreas, thus called pancreatic cancer. In those days they rarely mentioned the C word 'cancer'. Medical professionals let this dreaded disease remain unnamed, having no treatment or cure. My Mom's cancer wasn't named until it appeared on the autopsy report.

My mother expired, as they put it, at 2:35 PM on November 7, 1970. Obsessed with taping everything, Tommy, my younger brother, liked to tape record phone calls. This time, when he called the VA Hospital asking to speak to Ruby Freeborn, they told him Ruby Freeborn had expired at 2:35 PM.

I often wondered how my 13-year-old brother handled that news.

Upon my arriving home from work, Tommy gave me his tape player and said, "here listen to this!"

I said "no, not now. I have to call Dad in Albany, he'll need a ride home, he needs to get back to work soon."

The phone rang, it was Dad, "I'm glad you called," I said, "I was wondering how everything was up there."

"Your mother died," he said in a low voice.

"What?" I exclaimed. I felt sick, I wanted to do something, but nothing came to mind, I didn't have any words to say. My father was hurting, I could tell by the tone and tempo of his voice.

He continued, "The bus will be in Newburgh in about two hours, a little past 6 o'clock. Could you meet me at the station?" I said I'd be there.

Dad continued, "We will take care of everything when I get home, tell the kids, okay?" I agreed.

I hung the phone up in disbelief; I thought Mom was getting better; she was doing fine the doctor had told us. The trip to Albany was just a follow-up after the surgery at St. Luke's.

Tommy came into the kitchen, I had to tell him the news, should I wait until Dad gets home, I wondered? Dad told me to tell the kids, so I better do it. He had a strange look and I asked, "What's the matter?"

"Mom's dead," he said.

"How do you know?" I questioned.

"I have it here on my tape player, here listen." Tom hit the play button, I listened to the conversation he had earlier with the hospital person.

"Dad just told me; he's on his way home now. Tom, take it easy, Mom was suffering and now she's with God," I tried to explain.

He stomped out of the room mumbling something. I started after him, but he wanted to be alone. He needed time, his anger was always near the surface, but I knew he'd cool off. I'd give him his space now.

I heard Suzanne as she entered the kitchen. Her happy disposition, much like Mom's, always made me feel good, but not now.

"I have bad news," I blurted.

" What?" she questioned.

"Dad called me from Albany, Mom died this afternoon." My sister plopped down on a kitchen chair and began to cry.

I said, "Mom died peacefully, according to Dad. She suffered for a long time and now she was with Jesus." These words popped into my mind, I didn't know what else to say.

I stayed with her for a while; then she looked up and asked, "what time did it happened? Where was Dad when it happened?"

I told her I wasn't sure, but that Dad will be home soon.

"I have to run and get him in Newburgh." I asked her to look after Tommy.

"I will, I have to see him," she whispered.

I left the house to get Dad, I'd leave the call to Jeff (my older brother), to Dad, or I'd call him later.

I was in a daze as I drove to the bus station. I thought of my Mom lying somewhere on a slab of granite, or maybe in a dark locker. How awful, my mother was dead, and we were so far apart. I wished I had been there when she died. I needed to tell her I loved her once more. I needed a hug from her, and I needed her to tell me that everything would be all right. These selfish thoughts propelled me into this trancelike state. Nothing seemed real as I traveled the familiar roads and highways to the bus station.

The bus from Albany arrived a few minutes late. I couldn't wait to see Dad; maybe he could help us through this. He was strong and practical with lots of faith.

He looked haggard; his tieless shirt was open at the collar, not the way my father kept himself. He had been drinking while waiting for his bus. I recognize that glazed look on his face which usually showed his near intoxication. We exchange greetings as he got into the car; his face appeared red and flushed. I said nothing to him after our initial greeting. I started the car and headed home.

The ride home was quiet, my father inquired about my sister and brother. I asked him how he was doing; he shrugged and hung his head. He was hurting. I realized he could not help us right now; Dad needed to get himself together. As we turned onto Lattintown Road, he instructed me to make a stop; he needed cigarettes and/or a quart of Ballantine Ale.

Suzanne was waiting for us in the kitchen; she was putting something together for dinner. She gave Dad a big hug; they both were fighting back tears. I was filled with emotion as I watched them.

November 11, 1970 was a cold dreary damp day. The funeral home was making final arrangements to transport my mother's body to St. Mary's Church, a short distance from the funeral home.

The funeral director asked people to pay their last respects before going to their cars for the procession to the church. Soon the only people left in the room were my family, the 6 of us. This would be the last time we would all be face to face. My sister was weeping and her eyes seem to never stop tearing, I was an emotional basket case, I couldn't cry, I didn't want my Dad to see me cry. He had not cried, so why should I, men don't cry, I thought.

We all gathered around the casket surrounded with flowers and sympathy cards. We knelt down and said a prayer for the repose of my mother's soul. I prayed that God would receive her into heaven. My sister began to cry more out loud. My eyes filled with tears, but I fought them back.

We walked out of the funeral home and got in our car, leaving Dad alone to say his last goodbye. He had to look upon her face one more time; he had to tell her how much he loved her, and he always would. Death would not interfere with his love for her.

I sat motionless, waiting for Dad. He finally came out and got in the car. We watched them load my mother's body into the hearse. No one uttered a word. Then my Dad began to weep, he could no longer hold back his tears. His heart was broken. The weeping reminded me of an evening six years earlier, the night his mother died, he wept the same way, broken and hurt.

I fought back tears during the entire mass, the Catholic Rite of Christian burial. The words read spoke to my heart, helping to comfort me.

The Scripture reading spoke of eternal life. I am the way, the truth and the life, anyone who dies and believes in me, will have eternal life.

Heaven became a real place for me that day. It was, after all, the place in which my mother would spend eternity. We would be together again, someday, the priest said.

At the gravesite, Msgr. Simmons continued, "Death, where is your victory, where is your sting? Jesus has overcome death, through His resurrection, ashes to ashes and dust to dust; so we lay Ruby here in this resting place. Her soul will not stay here. He promised she will be delivered unto the Lord Jesus. Her earthly body will pass away, and she will be given a new body, perfect and free from sickness and never to die again. In heaven, Ruby will be with the Angels and the Saints, where someday we will all be together."

That was His promise, but I had a hard time with the fact my mother would be put in a 6-foot deep hole in the ground. She deserved better than that, she didn't like cold damp places. I tried to tell myself she's not there; she was en-route to heaven. This is where reality and spirituality collided for me. I had to become less realistic and more spiritual to understand what was happening. I grew older that day, and the thought of my mother in that grave would haunt me for years to come.

Chapter 3

I walked awkwardly toward the chopper pad, trying to adjust the weight of the rucksack. The whine of the chopper got my attention; guess they saw us coming. The helicopter seemed huge as it sat there waiting. The rotor blades were at least 12 feet above ground, yet everyone ducked. The pad, made of corrugated steel, had a target painted on it to assist setting down the chopper. A chopper pilot, wearing a flight suit and helmet, met us.

He instructed us to get in and hold on. "I may need to drop you in, the gunner will tell you when to jump. I'll get as low as I can. Head over to the chopper, we're ready to go, good luck," he concluded.

We followed him and pulled ourselves through the large open side door. Once in, the chopper lifted and banked hard; then straightened out. The nose of the chopper lowered, and it picked up speed. What a strange sensation, hanging in mid-air. My heart pounded until I got adjusted. I kept thinking of jumping out of this thing with an 80 pound rucksack and my M-16 locked and loaded. Welcome to Vietnam, I was on edge and just scared enough to keep my wits about me. I looked down at open fields with lots of water and marshland. We were up a few thousand feet, safe from small arms fire. The door gunner studied the land below; if the chopper got fired on, he would respond with his tripod mounted machine gun, an awesome weapon.

As the chopper descended, I caught sight of red smoke off in the distance; I wondered what it was. When the pilot saw smoke, he headed for it and set the chopper down. Later I was told, they used colored smoke for verification, the chopper pilots would confirm the smoke color by radio. Sometimes Charlie (VC) would try to confuse the landing by popping their own smoke canister; they never knew what color, so it was hit and miss.

This was not the case today. With smoke confirmed, the chopper headed to the designated LZ. There were men positioned around the LZ, low to the ground with weapons. I made it to the open door and scooted out. Upon hitting the soft marshy reed grass, I stumbled. Pulling myself up, I moved away from the ascending helicopter. In a split second, I found myself crouched down in the middle of reed grass. The other guys were nearby, and the chopper was gone. Let's move someone said; right there was the grunt that popped smoke and guided the chopper to the LZ. We followed him as he made his way to the perimeter where the scene took on a different look.

Our Company Commander (CO) Captain Mac (McDaniels) met us and assigned us to squads.

"Freeborn," he barked, "go with Steele."

Sgt. Steele waived, and I moved toward him. "The squad was setting up the NDP (night-time defensive position), and we won't be digging in, we may leave here sooner than expected. I want you to stay near Pogo (Van Hall) pointing to a thin, curly-haired guy. If you need anything, he can square you away. I'll be back TT." (Slang we used meaning in a hurry or soon).

Pogo was busy setting up, I asked, "where do you want me to set up?"

He pointed to an area next to his, "set up here," he said.

I dropped my ruck, and he extended his hand,

"Hey, I'm Pogo."

"Joe, nice to meet you," I replied.

After fumbling with my rucksack, I got my bedding and mess stuff out, selected a few cans of c-rats, it appeared to be dinner time. I noticed guys heating items up on what looked like a little burner.

Pogo came over and said, "it's C4, I'll show you how we do it."

He pulled out a used brick of C4, a plastic explosive, enough to level an average house or small building. He picked off a piece, the size of a dime, and lit it with his Zippo lighter.

"This will burn for 10 or 15 minutes, put it under this burner," he instructed. He handed me a blackened c-rat can, with holes in it. "It's a home-made burner, we all use them. Put the c-rat can you want to heat on top of the burner, in TT it will be hot."

Pogo turned back and said, "Oh, don't stomp on C4 when it's burning, it can take off your fuckin foot. It will detonate upon impact. Take any C4 residue, Charlie will be in here tomorrow pickin' up this area. He'll use your leftover shit to kill you, booby-traps, remember?"

Something I heard in my in-country training, I'd be careful not to leave anything.

I finished cleaning up the C4 residue, putting the charred remains in a plastic bag and secured it in my ammo box. I'd dispose of it later.

Sgt. Steele came by with more instructions. "You'll have guard duty between 2 and 3 AM. You will relieve Hud (Bill Hudson); I'll bring him over later. No smoking or igniting matches or lighters while on duty, you will have a nighttime sighting device and you will man the pig (the M-60 machine gun)."

Steele continued, "The CP guard will check on you a few times during your shift. He will warn you with the following signal, Green Light. That means he's coming your way. It will be in the form of a loud whisper, so be listening for it. If you hear movement near your location, quietly say, halt, who goes there. The response should be Green Light. I will be at the next NDP just past the guard location, if you as much as hear a twig snap, I want you to wake my ass up. I'm not taking any chances. You'll get used to the freaky noises out here, but it'll take a while."

"Hey Hud, this is Freeborn, he got in today, you'll be getting his ass up for guard duty."

"Welcome to the bush," Hud sneered, "where ya from?"

40

I told him, "New York."

"Utah," he said. I extended my hand to shake his, he grabbed my thumb and palm "this is how we do it over here."

We talked more, then Steele and Hud left.

It was getting dark, and I needed to get familiar with my immediate area. Moving around inside the NDP, I observed about 30 guys in the platoon consisting of 3 squads and the CP (command post). The CP was set up in the middle of the NDP, with the squads surrounding them in a circular perimeter. Each squad would man the 3 DPs (defensive positions). Everyone would pull guard duty for one hour.

I returned to my position, and got everything set for a good night's sleep, yeah right. I wouldn't sleep a wink, knowing I had to get up at 2 AM. However I needed to try, I'd be humping tomorrow. I took my boots off, crawled into the poncho liner and closed my eyes.

"Psst, hey Freeborn, let's go, I'm tired man I need to get some Z's." What, where am I, what the hell, then it hit me. Bush.... guard duty, oh yeah.

"Is that you Hud?"

"Yeah, who do you think it is? Get over to the DP."

I pulled on my boots, grabbed my fatigue shirt and my M-16, and felt my way over to what I remember to be the way. At first, I thought I was lost. Where the hell am I? It was pitch black, much darker than when I came by earlier. I wondered if I was going in the right direction; then, just ahead I saw the pig sitting there like I remembered.

I cleared the sleep from my eyes and tried to focus in the darkness. The minutes seemed like hours, and I kept checking the time. My eyes now adjusted to the darkness, I could see my immediate area better. I looked through the nighttime sighting device a few times; it was a dull green image, and I had to study the images to understand what I was seeing. After a while I could identify trees, bushes, rocks, etc..

Soon I would wake Pogo to relieve me. I waited until 3 AM, then made my way back to Pogo's position. He was sound asleep.

"It's your turn," I said.

"Yeah thanks," he replied.

I made my way back to my NDP, pulled off my boots, tucked my M-16 in and drifted off to sleep.

The commotion woke me; I heard guys moving around, packing up, fumbling with mess kits and canteen cups. Several little c-rats cans, smoking and burning C4, greeted my senses. It was morning, time to get up.

An older guy came over to my position, "hey man, you got a pound cake?" he asked.

"Pound cake?" I questioned.

"Yeah you know, c-rats, pound cake," he shot back.

I wasn't sure what I had. The supply Sgt. had given us a variety of boxed c-rat cans; I hadn't time to check them out as yet.

"I'll look," I said.

Fumbling with my rucksack, I pulled out some cans, and the guy said, "there's one," he motioned. I handed it to him.

"Pudgy's (Robert Angus) my name," he announced with a wide grin.

"Joe," I replied.

"Cool man," he said as he left.

I continued to pull my gear together and pack my rucksack for the long day of humping. As I packed up, I remember thinking I've met about half of my squad so far. Pogo and Hud were fairly new grunts, and I'm glad I met them. Then my mind drifted back to my recent encounter with Pudgy. A strange guy, older than most of us, but I liked him. He seemed carefree and comfortable in Nam. It was way too early to draw any conclusions, but I was glad I had these first few encounters with these guys. They would be very influential in the next few months of my tour.

I was finishing up when Steele and a few guys I hadn't met, came over to my location.

Steele announced, "this is Freeborn, your newbie squad member. Keep an eye on him today, we need to keep him around for a while," he joked. "Okay, let's pack up, we're movin' out on patrol in about 10 minutes."

Patrol, what does that mean? I didn't remember any specific training on patrolling. Steele and the rest of the squad fell in line. Pudgy, the designated point man, Reese (Reese Merrill) his slack man, lined up first. I was midway in the lineup. The pig gunner and his assistant were behind me. The rest were riflemen and filled in between us. We moved out, leaving 3 or 4 feet between each man. As I left the NDP, I wondered what was in store for me today. Stray thoughts came in my mind, but I dismiss them, concentrating on the task at hand, my first patrol.

Where was the rest of the platoon? I assumed they were nearby or just behind us. My assumption was correct; they had formed similar lines and were behind us. As the terrain changed, I could see the long line of troops behind us. It was comforting to see these guys, knowing most had lots of field experience. I needed to keep myself calm and focused on the business of the day, survival.

After an hour of humping, the guy in front of me turned around and whispered "break." I instinctively turned to the guy behind me and repeated, "break." I squatted and leaned back and used my rucksack as a backrest. I reached into my shirt pocket and pulled out my smokes. This routine would become common over the next months in Nam.

I sat there taking in my surroundings; the foliage and the plants; things looked nice out here. It was early morning, the grass and leaves were still wet from dew. There were lots of bird noises and small crawling insects all around me. I remember the Company Clerk's warning about leeches; I checked my bloused pant legs.

"Let's go man," the guy in front of me grunted, "we're moving out." The guys behind me were getting up and soon we were all moving again.

Before long I noticed the guys in front of me and the guys behind me. To my surprise Pogo was two positions behind me and then came Hud, who was in front of the assistant pig gunner, followed by the pig (M-60 machine gun) gunner. I spotted Steele behind the pig gunner and I was getting a sense of organization.

Our surroundings were always changing; we would go from thick jungle, to rocky clearings, through streambeds, then back to wooded areas. As we proceeded, my mind would wander.

Suddenly, gunfire. I saw the guys ahead of me falling to the ground and I hit the deck. "Ambush!" someone yelled, we were being fired on. The VC (Viet Cong) had been waiting for us on higher ground, and as we passed through this low trail, all hell broke loose. Our pig gunner set down the M-60 and began laying down heavy fire. I noticed my squad moving up to higher ground out of the low ditch.

Amid all the confusion, Pogo grabbed my arm and yelled, "you do everything I do."

Without hesitation I followed him up the embankment to the wooded area where this war started for me. The small arms fire, the machine gun fire, it was an unimaginable scene.

By this time the enemy, the VC and NVA (North Vietnamese Army) troops, had suffered casualties. The VC had positioned themselves in trees and higher locations making them easy targets. The shit had hit the fan, and I was in the middle of it. Pogo stayed close and instructed me through the firefight. I'm not sure how long it lasted, but the carnage was significant. After a while, someone shouted "cease-fire, cease-fire, cease-fire." In an instant all was quiet. We were all on edge not knowing what was coming. As we carefully made our way through the ambush site, we observed VC and NVA killed or wounded. I never fired my weapon.

It was over. The shooting, the confusion and the immediate danger had passed. Now we had to care for our wounded. I was in a state of shock; just going through the motions as I followed Pogo's instructions. Steele and some other guys had assembled to figure out our next move. The rest of the platoon was now in place, our CP (command post) was busy calling in air strikes and communicating with the rear area. We took prisoners and transported the VC casualties to another location. Before any of this would happen however, choppers would land and take our wounded to the 95th EVAC hospital at China Beach.

After a while we were back on patrol, still numb and in disbelief, I had to keep calm and focus on the mission. I had survived this one.

My thoughts now drifted to my non-existent relationship with Jesus; it had to become personal. I'd been struggling with the fear of death and entered Nam doubting I would make it out alive. I had just witnessed men who I didn't know get killed or wounded. These guys were well-trained and they should have survived. I had no illusions of my survival, death seemed eminent. These thoughts stayed with me the rest of that day.

We stopped for lunch and to regroup. The AO (area of operation) was clear with no enemy activity. As we sat there opening c-rat cans and other foodstuffs, the atmosphere was somber. We did not assemble in groups. In the bush each man was self-sufficient. He carried his own food, his own water, his own smokes, for a good reason. The term we used was 'Cluster Fuck' (or Charlie Foxtrot). This was when troops got too close together during maneuvers in the bush. Charlie was always watching, at least that is how we conducted ourselves in the bush. This lunch break was a solitary time for me.

We moved out and continue our patrol. Walking several more hours looking for an enemy we couldn't see. At sunset we headed towards our designated NDP. Our radio operator had received the location where the Company would meet.

Guys were digging in when we arrived. The VC liked to attack at night; believing darkness gave them the best chance of overrunning our position. Taking extra precautions, we would dig foxholes tonight, and set up extra ordinances outside our NDP. Tripwires attached to Claymore mines, attached to flares, attached to grenades, were all part of our nighttime defensive position. We would remain extra vigilant this evening, dug in and ready for anything. Pogo explained all this as we set up our position. He would set up right next to me to keep an eye on me. His concern was not for me, but for the Company and for his survival. In the bush we had to keep our emotions and fears in check. The unit could not tolerate guys who were nervous or scared. Being a newbie, I was well trained, mentally and physically strong, I had to keep it together.

I didn't rest easy that night, and I prayed a lot. I confronted Jesus about wanting this personal relationship with Him. I told Him I wanted that close relationship; I wanted Him as a friend. Immediately something happened, it's hard to explain, but Jesus spoke to me spiritually and told me whatever happens, I am there with you. And if you get injured or killed, I will be with you. Jesus' message was profound; and came out of nowhere.

Remember earlier in this story, the "born again"? This was my first encounter with Christ.

I drifted off to sleep secure in knowing Jesus was there with me in Vietnam, and would stay with me for the rest of my life. In that knowledge death was no longer scary. I had Jesus' promise (of eternal life), everything would be okay. Jesus further instructed me to pray. Praying wasn't part of my daily routine, I remembered the Lord's Prayer, the Hail Mary, the Act of Contrition and some other prayers. Then, to my surprise, the 23rd Psalm came to my mind.....

The Lord is my shepherd; I have everything I need.

He lets me rest in fields of green grass and he leads me to quiet pools of fresh water.

He gives me new strength. He guides me in the right paths as he has promised.

Even if I go through the deepest darkness, I will not be afraid, Lord you are with me.

Your shepherd's rod and staff protect me.

You prepare a banquet for me where all my enemies can see me; you welcome me as an honored guest and fill my cup filled to the brim.

And your goodness and your love will be with me all my life;

and your house will be my home as long as I live.

I found the 23rd Psalm in my bible and read it several times. This was the prayer Jesus wanted me to pray, it was the promise of eternal life.

I drifted off to sleep that night feeling as if God was holding me in the palm of his hand, knowing no harm would come to me. Jesus was with me leading me home, in his way, in his time. I had a life changing experience that mid-August day in 1971.

I prayed the 23rd Psalm day and night. When I got scared, I would pray all the more. In my prayerfulness, I would feel the Lord's hand on me, sometimes pushing me; other times pulling me through difficult situations during my entire tour of duty.

This night was quiet and guard duty was not the chore it had been. I was wide awake and eager to protect our NDP. I noticed more motion within the NDP and radio messages being received and transmitted from the CP. We were all on edge and morning couldn't come soon enough.

It was about 3 AM when I returned from the guard position; I drifted off for a few minutes, but never really fell asleep. At day break I noticed how serine and peaceful things seemed.

"Hey Freeborn," Pogo said, "we're moving out in 15, get your shit together and come over by me TT!"

I jumped up, pulled on my boots, and packed everything away. Pogo was on the perimeter, picking up the ordinance we set out the night before. In a few minutes, we were humping down the side of a hill, slipping and trying not to fall, the grade was steep and slick from the early morning dew.

After several hours of humping over hill and dale, taking care to keep our location from the VC, we arrived just below a fire base, at Marble Mountain. They used this strategic site, well-guarded and secure, to move troops in and out of this AO. Steele told us to break, and we took positions around the LZ watching choppers land and take off.

After about an hour our resupply chopper landed, they had clean clothes, more rations, soda, beer and letters from home. This wasn't a scheduled resupply; our CO thought it would cheer us up while we waited for further mission instructions.

Large duffel bags of tee shirts, socks, fatigue shirts and pants would be rummaged through. Guys would find their size; grab socks and underwear and anything else they needed. The mess Sergeant served us hot chow. We got 2 cans of soda (pop) and 1 can of Schaffer (beer).

Mike, the Company Clerk announced "mail-call" and read off names. Guys gathered around. I held back, never thinking he'd call me.

"Freeborn," Mike barked. I got up and moved over to his position; I received my first letter from home.

August 27, 1971

Hi Joey,

We got your second letter today, so it doesn't take too long. We hadn't written because you said the address was not permanent.

Sure was glad to hear you are all right and in with a good unit, this can be a big help to be with someone who knows what they're doing. The allotment came about a week ago, if you need more money over there, cut the amount down, don't go without anything, and we want to know what you can use and send packages every couple of weeks, but we would like to know what's hard to get there and anything else that you might want.

Everything is about the same here just going to work and thinking of getting Tom back to school. Suzanne is out tonight on another bridal thing this weekend, but she too was just waiting to get your address. I'll also send it to Pauline and Marie and Uncle Allen.

I hope you had good luck on your first mission and remember what I told you not to trust any of them, the

"Cowboys" will be a good indication of how these people are. Don't trust any of them at any age.

We had quite a bit of rain today, part of a hurricane that is due to hit along the coast about midnight tonight, we don't expect it to come this far inland tho.

I saw Angie and her mother at the store a week or so before they left for Italy and she said you had her address and would be in touch with her over in Europe.

We haven't had a ride in Harry's boat yet, it seems they blew a head gasket on the trip and have been working now building a trailer to move it back out of the water. That sure was a short summer for the boat. They bought a burnt-out house trailer for $400 and scrapped it to get at the frame, after a lot of welding and whatnot it should be ready in a month.

Get to church as often as you can, I suppose mass is said in the field, but keep your faith and I'm sure all will be okay. We'll be praying for you and I'll have Sister Mary Margaret at Mount St. Mary's remember you. I'm enclosing a bookmark she sent to me, I think it's encouraging.

It's late now so I'll get this off to you and write again in a couple of days. We're all with you, so have courage.

Love Dad.

I read the letter over a few times, making sure I got everything straight in my mind. I worried about how my Dad was taking my being in Nam. I tried to read between the lines, and I came away with him being upbeat, I guess that's all I could hope for.

The rest of the day dragged, we had to keep our shit tight, ready to move out. Where I wondered, but dismissed any feelings of anxiety or fear.

Chapter 4

I was 12 years old the day John F. Kennedy was assassinated. It was November 22, 1963. Two years later, Kennedy's successor, Lyndon Johnson decided to heat up the war in Southeast Asia. He escalated the war by sending more troops, Marines primarily. Johnson, like Kennedy, believed that Vietnam would be the line that Communism would not cross. At the time Communism was on the advance, Cuba had just fallen and more countries would fall if the United States and their allies did not stop the "domino effect" of Communism. JFK wasn't clear on his position regarding Southeast Asia before his assignation. Some historians said he was a "Cold Warrior President" and would use military force to stop the spread of Communism. Others weren't sure. History can only speculate what JFK would have done.

In the mid 60's I paid little or no attention to world affairs. I heard comments like we had to stop the commie aggression. My Dad believed Communism would take over Asia and then infiltrate Europe if left unchecked. We had to take a stand, and that justified this undeclared war in Vietnam, at least that's what he thought. I still wasn't sure.

I entered Marlboro Central High School in 1965 with friends I had known since kindergarten. It seemed we'd always been together and shared many experiences. My older brother and sister were attending the same high school, which made my transition easier.

While in Vietnam I often recalled these times and my friends. Their letters took on an important role while in Nam. Let me introduce you to some of them.

Joe Ferrari, we called him "Fuzz", and he was my closest and dearest friend. I recall his mother once introducing me as Joseph's friend, from that time on, Fuzz was my friend, his mother had said so.

Ed Pross, we called him "Eddie Que" or "Que-ball", a happy-go-lucky guy, with a big friendly smile. He loved cars, racing and anything that went fast. If it had two wheels and a motor, he would try it out on his make shift racetrack behind his house. We spent many after school hours working on either an old VW, motorcycle, mini-bike or go-cart, anything with wheels and a motor.

Annette Mannese, a new friend. She had attended another school until high school, she was always friendly, and kept us informed of what was happening. I sometimes found her playfully annoying, but I always liked her.

Angie Marcon, Annette's best friend, was a quiet girl, with long blond hair, big blue eyes and always proper. She seemed different from other girls I knew. I liked her, and looked forward to stopping by her table during lunch. She disapproved of my cigarette smoking and my other bad boy habits, but she always seemed amused by my antics. We started dating in January of 1969.

Lorraine Rodelli, Annette's cousin and a good friend. They had attended school together, and she too was new to our school. Lorraine was friendly and funny, and she, like Annette, kept us informed. She was also a bit of a matchmaker. If the guys wanted to explore the possibility of taking a girl out, we would ask Lorraine to inquire if this would be possible. That way guys wouldn't be embarrassed if they got rejected. This came in very handy in high school.

In this chapter you'll read letters from these friends. They tried to keep me positive and encouraged me, filling me in on things going on back home. These letters gave me hope which I'd hold on to month after month after month.

I always welcomed the letters from home from Dad and my sister. I wrote to my younger brother Tommy, he wrote me once. I never received a letter from my older brother Jeff. There may have been several reasons he didn't write, maybe he didn't want to face the fact his kid brother was in Vietnam. He had avoided the draft (flat feet). I think it scared him to even imagine me there, so he went about his life.

Jeff was five years my senior, and was a hippie type, free spirit, having grown up in the early 60s. He experienced the Cultural Revolution first hand and was involved in what was happening. In July 1969 he attended the Woodstock Music Festival. That was the 'Summer of Love' and he sure enjoyed the concert, after which he grew his hair longer and wore shabby clothes.

In 1970 Jeff opened a head-shop. He sold various leather goods, clothing, boots, novelty items, etc. He also sold legal drug paraphernalia such as water pipes, incense, hash pipes and other items used to smoke marijuana and hashish. Jeff came of age at the beginning of the Vietnam War; he graduated high school in 1964. His perspective of the war differed from mine.

His political views were out there and was against the war in Vietnam.

My Dad would go on and on how Communism had to be stopped; LBJ was right in my father's opinion. Even though Dad was a Conservative Republican, he agreed with LBJ's proliferation of the war and the efforts by the Armed Forces, which he held in the highest esteem. My Dad, a World War II veteran, flew missions on B-17s over Germany and occupied France. After 8 successful missions his plane was shot down, parachuted out of the aircraft, was captured and held as POW in Germany. Eventually he was liberated and returned home. Upon his return, he got busy living his life; he got married and raised his family. He never discussed the war years, at least not with me. When he talked about the Vietnam War however, he would get my attention. I thought he knew what he was talking about.

When my turn came to serve in Vietnam, I had mixed emotions. My father, more for the war than against it, but by 1969-1970 things changed. The anti-war protesters had gotten a lot of traction, the effort was lost they said and there was no victory to be had in Vietnam. The protesters had the evening news monopolized, and their message was reaching more and more people. My father wondered why we would fight a war we had no plans to win. He was changing, now questioning what he once thought to be noble and just.

In reality by 1969 the war had become too costly, and could no longer be justified. Our mission was unclear and victory allusive.

When I was drafted in 1971, they used the Lottery to pick the next crop of young recruits to proliferate this war. In December 1970 my number was 52, out of 365. In early February 1971 I received my draft notice. The letter started, "Greeting" and instructed, I was to report to the induction center in Kingston, New York on March 3, 1971 to begin my Basic Training in the U.S. Army. I studied the letter and wondered why me, why now. I was out of high school, I completed one year of college, I had a job, I had a steady girlfriend, I had a nice car and despite all that, this induction notice would change everything. The first feeling I had was fear of going overseas and having to fight a war that had become very unpopular.

More of my friends were now voicing their opposition to the Vietnam War. This war became real to us when L.Cpl. William (Boo) Partington (our friend) was killed in action in 1970. He was one of two men from our small town to die in Vietnam.

It was time to voice my opposition to this war, but the government had other plans for me.

While in Nam, the letters I received from my friends helped keep me in touch with things familiar; they reminded me of events and activities a million miles away. Their letters brought me back to those happy times; reminding me this was not permanent. They gave me hope when there didn't seem to be any. These simple and sometimes silly letters kept me going while in Vietnam.

Oh, my nickname in high school was Flea. I never liked it, but it stuck and everyone called me that.

The 1st letter

September 17, 1971

Dear Flea,

Hi! I received your letter today and was very happy to hear from you.

Right now I am anxiously awaiting Angie's return. I am really surprised that she hasn't written to me in quite a while. I only received one letter from her and that was soon after she left. I don't even know when she is returning. I am really sorry to hear that your letters don't reach her. I'm sure she is dying to hear from you.

I am also sorry to hear you are real lonely and feeling a bit depressed. I guess I expected that and all I can say Flea is try to bear it. As you said you only have 10 months more and I know that seems like a lifetime right now, but it really isn't. There's not much us folks at home can do, except pray for you and keep writing. I know that's not much, but it's something. I'm also glad that you finally wrote it like it is! Usually in your letters you're always sounding so cheerful, and I know deep down you didn't feel that way. I'm always pouring out my troubles to you so once in a while give it back to me.

I also feel a sense of responsibility with my job. It's good to be earning my own pay and doing as I please with it.

Flea, you know what kind of friend I consider you. You are the only male person to whom I feel I can talk things over with, my problems especially. I always feel that the advice you give me is wise and good. And I also think you're a great person besides! That's why I'm glad that you and Ang are together. You are both great people and I know you will be very happy for your entire life together.

Well Flea, I'll shut up now nothing new has been happening around here.

Oh, Joanne Rodelli and Harry Eckert got engaged last Wednesday. Isn't that nice! As for me, no news!!! No luck!!

Well Flea, I intended on writing you a nice long letter in a few days. It so happens that the day I bought this card I received your letter. So until then stay well be good and have faith.

Love Ya, Annette.

PS. Don't forget to write when you get a chance you are always in my thoughts.

This letter, the first from Annette, inspired her boyfriend, Fuzz to write. The next letter from Fuzz gave me a different perspective on what was going on back home.

September 16, 1971

Hi Flea,

*How the #%@*are you. I am sad that I didn't write sooner but I'm really in a bind at Dutchess. At this moment I am sitting in my evening class, Business 244. This is my* first night class, and this is a real bummer. It lasts for three hours, 7 PM to 10 PM. This teacher is putting me to sleep. So how are things in the Far East? It must be a bad trip for you. I really feel for you, no shit.

I quit working for Royal Tire Service "#%@*work". Turtle is still working there for a while. I guess Angie is due back from Europe soon. I hope she had a wonderful time. I hope someday that I can go to Europe, because Marlboro sucks.

I hear that Joe Noto will be joining you shortly in Nam. So what do you do on Friday and hey, is it true that most of the GI's over there smoke pot regularly? What's the Saturday nights like? Shack up with some Vietnamese Hummer or just trip out?

Mouse lost a lot of weight and is still screwing off. The trend at Dutchess is bra-less, I can't look at all the snakes here because I'll lose my mind. All those jugs just a bouncin stimulates me.

If you need anything, just let me know and we'll send it to you. Well, got to go! Take care Pal!

Be cool Fuzz.

PS. You should see Eddie Que's Chevy powered Buick, Grand Sport. He did one of his quickie jobs, his *brother 'Yon-Yon' helped him with the interior. The first night he got it on the road he came out by 'Panzies' and powered second and blew the driveshaft right out from under the car.*

I found this letter to be humorous and allowed me a mental reprieve from this place. Fuzz wrote this as if he was speaking to me. It was like we were together. I missed the expressions on his face and the laughter we'd share. Most of this letter was nonsense, but up to now most of my life was nonsense.

September 27, 1971, Monday 9:30 PM

Dear Flea,

Hi, how have you been? I hope you have been okay, considering where you are! Everything here is about the same as when I wrote you last. You should have received a letter from Fuzz because I mailed it a week ago. I'm glad he finally got to write you. I also gave your address to Mouse and Pat, so you will probably be hearing from them soon!

Right now, I have just finished doing some homework for Fuzz, the things I don't do for Him!!

I also just finished talking to Ang for about an hour. It seems we could talk all night! She was also writing you a letter which I was glad about. Today was her first day at work and she's dead tired! She'll probably tell you all about it, so I'll skip that!

Well work for me has been okay nothing new has been happening. Things with Fuzz and me have been good, so nothing to complain about to you, Flea!

Guess what, I saw "The Night of the Living Dead" Friday night, I went to see it with Fuzz, of course, and Lorraine and Richie, Harry and Joanne. We all went in Harry's station wagon to the drive-in, so you can imagine what went on. Between Harry and Fuzz scaring the hell out of us girls and Joanne and Lorraine screaming every five minutes, the night was pretty scary. It was good but I really would have liked to see it alone so I could've gotten the real affect. And as usual, we miss the beginning so I missed the best parts!

I got the white stripe painted on my car, Flea. It looks pretty good. The best part is I didn't pay a penny for it. A friend of my brother did it for me. Of course I gave him a gift, but I didn't have to pay $25 or $50 for it. It seems my car goes faster now with the stripe on! Or maybe it's just in my head! Ha Ha. My car has been running okay, so far. I'll have to give it a good tune up for the winter and buy snow tires and I'll be all set!

Well Flea, it's getting late and I've got to get to bed. I just wanted to say hello and let you know that I am always thinking about you and praying for you. Don't ever think you are forgotten because Ang and I talk about you constantly. I consider you my best friend also, remember that.

Please write me because you know I love hearing from you. It always makes me feel good! Also, Flea, if anything is bothering you let off some steam in a letter to me. I feel good when I know you're telling it like it really is. So write me and let me know how things are.

I will write again soon Flea until then take care of yourself and be good. We all love you here.

Love, Annette.

I received this letter in early October 1971. I was more comfortable in my unit and in the bush. I had not received a letter from Angie, but this letter indicated that one was on its way. It was good to read 'I was not forgotten' in this letter. At times in Vietnam I felt isolated and alone. These letters helped chase those feelings away.

Chapter 5

The headlines back home read "The Americal 1st Battalion, 46th Infantry, and attached units sustained the single largest American loss of the year." I didn't even know it happened that March day, 1971. I had just entered the service and was in Basic Training in Ft. Dix, New Jersey; all news from the outside had stopped. This was the beginning of my lost year. Many things happened that I never knew about. This significant and tragic story is one example.

NOTE: I italicize my comments which are not part of the original article.

"Sixty Minutes Of Terror At Mary Ann"

By Al Hemingway

"Most of us didn't talk about it when we came home," said Ed Newton of Sawyer, Kan., and a veteran of the 46th Infantry. "In my opinion, the media blew it all out of proportion when they mentioned the drugs and sleeping on duty. It's time we set the record straight and tell the truth about Mary Ann." *Indeed, it is.*

In the early morning hours of March 28, 1971, an estimated 50 sappers from the 2nd Co., 409th (VC) Main Force Sapper Battalion quietly neared their objective-- Fire Support Base (FSB) Mary Ann—a remote outpost of the 196th Light Inf. Bde. (LIB), 23rd Infantry (American) Div., located in the western highlands of Quang Tin province in Military Region I of South Vietnam.

Precarious Position

Mary Ann's purpose was to provide a protective shield for Da Nang and other costal hamlets. Also, it was a jumping-off point for operations designed to disrupt the flow of men and material coming down the Dak Rose Trail.

The 196th Light Infantry Brigade, 23rd American Division was responsible for the security and manning of this outpost, strategic to their area of operation (AO). In six months, I would join this unit. They changed the name of the unit from the Americal Division to the 46th Infantry Division. Nothing else changed, their mission continued unaffected. Originally, I entered in-country orientation in an Americal unit, and wore the distinctive Americal patch for a short while before my arrival in Da Nang.

While my attention to events in Vietnam was limited prior to my induction into the Army, I had heard of the Americal

Division because of 2nd Lt. Calley who had been front page news for months. He was responsible for the largest breach of military conduct in the history of the Vietnam war.

I thought at the time Americal was dropped because of the conviction of 2nd Lt. Calley, and for no other reason. But maybe the 30 American lives lost on March 28, 1971 on that dusty hill called Mary Ann may have been the deciding factor. Americal was a disgraced unit name. Further outrage and accusations about the over running of Mary Ann was all this once proud unit could take. War is unfair and unpredictable. We tried our best in a bad situation.

Erected on top of a ridge, it "occupied two camel humps with a shallow saddle in between." A series of ridges and hills enveloped the outpost on three sides, and thick jungle obscured the field of observation. Described as a "shanty-town," 30 hootches, bunkers and other buildings were sprinkled over its interior. The base was 546 yards in length, 82 yards wide across its saddle and 136 yards wide at both ends.

Twenty-two bunkers, constructed from metal conex shipping boxes, were placed around the outer perimeter. Most of the headquarters buildings were situated on the southeast side of the base: the Battalion Tactical Operations Center (BTOC), company command post (CP), communications bunker, a sensor monitoring station, ammunition storage bunkers, three mess halls, artillery liaison center, battalion aid station and fuel storage area.

The northwest end of the camp held two 155mm howitzer parapets, the fire direction center and the artillery CP. Also, a quad .50-caliber machine gun team was placed along the perimeter together with a detachment from a searchlight unit.

One line company from the 196th LIB was rotated from the field to Mary Ann approximately every two weeks and was responsible for its security while there.

For me, my time spent on another firebase, Linda, was like R&R, a break from the intensity I felt while in the bush. A shower, hot food, and guard duty at night, for a couple of weeks, helped to keep me going. I was there several times.

On the Perimeter

In all, 231 Americans and 21 South Vietnamese (ARVN) soldiers defended Mary Ann on that fateful night. Among them were the 75-man C Co., 1st Bn., 46th Inf.; an 18-man recon platoon; 34 medics, communications personnel, clerks and cooks from HQ Company; and an eight-man contingent from the 4.2-inch mortar platoon of E Company.

That crew was there assembling the remainder of the mortar ammo to take to FSB Mildred. (No heavy mortars were present that night on Mary Ann. Two mortars were sent to Chu Lai for repair, and the other two went to Mildred.)

There, too, were 81mm mortar crews from B and D companies; 20 men of 1st Plt., C btry., 3rd Bn., 16th FA, manning two 155mm howitzers; and artillerymen from four other units. Finally, 22 grunts from A, B and D companies were in transit.

Mary Ann had been spared an all-out attack. With the war winding down, no one believed the VC would hit such an insignificant outpost. "There was a false sense of security at Mary Ann," said John Pastrick, an infantryman with C Co., 1st Bn., 46th Inf. "It was very lax all the time."

But on this fog-shrouded evening, 50 VC sappers, their bodies covered with charcoal and grease to make them more difficult targets in the darkness, quietly slipped through Mary Ann's perimeter. Crouching low in three- to six-man teams, they made their way through the base's unsuspecting defenders.

Struck With a Vengeance

They wasted no time. Under the protective umbrella of a mortar barrage, sappers struck the vulnerable BTOC with a vengeance. Lt. Col. William P. Doyle, the battle-hardened battalion commander, was awakened when 82mm mortar shells landed with a resounding thud just outside his bunker.

To make matters worse, the sappers tossed CS (tear) gas into the BTOC. Chocking and unable to see, Doyle was knocked down when a satchel charge exploded. Regaining his composure, he drew his .45 pistol and pumped a round into a sapper's chest just before another satchel charge was heaved at him.

The force of that explosion threw him to the ground, leaving him unconscious. Coming to, Doyle struggled to stand up, only to have a third explosion go off in the BTOC. As a result, Doyle was again knocked out. He eventually made his way out of the burning BTOC and linked up with Capt. Paul S. Spilberg, who had choppered into Mary Ann several days before with a three-man training team from Chu Lai.

Spilberg had written that he was "so proud of my men I could burst. When we were without food and it was cold and pouring down rain... there was good humor and the highest degree of cooperativeness. The grunts were clean in the jungle—no drugs." He earned his third Purple Heart on Mary Ann.

While the BTOC was being destroyed, C Company's CP also was being hit hard. Capt. Richard V. Knight, the company's popular commander, was killed outright. 1st Lt. Daniel J. Mack, executive officer, was struck in the right leg by an AK-47 round, shredding his calf muscles. He feigned death while a sapper ripped the watch off his wrist.

Spec. 4 Carl D. Carter, a radio operator, was buried under sandbags when a wall of the bunker collapsed on him. He went undetected as the VC sprayed the room with automatic weapons fire.

Not so lucky was Sgt. Ronald J. Becksted, an easygoing NCO, who was killed instantly as he tried to escape the CP. Spec. 4 Thomas Simmons also was gunned down, but survived.

Staff Sgt. John C. Calhoun was hit three times and was lying near Pfc. Michael S. Holloway, who was frantically trying to tie a tourniquet on Calhoun's leg. As enemy sappers approached, both faked death. Calhoun survived, but Holloway was killed. As the VC moved on, one let loose a burst and Calhoun was wounded two more times.

Mary Ann was struck with such ferocity that its defenders were unable to mount any type of counterattack. Many grunts, who were asleep in their hootches, were either shot trying to escape or buried alive when the satchel charges were hurled into their quarters.

Mounting Resistance

A few soldiers managed to avoid the initial onslaught. Tripping over the body of a dead sapper in the confusion, Spec 4 David Tarnay picked up his AK-47. As he carefully maneuvered about, he saw an enemy soldier in the wire attempting to leave. Tarnay took careful aim, killing him.

Sgt. Maj. Carl N. Prosser and Pfc. John A. Bruno killed another sapper trying to flee the area. When the VC returned fire, Prosser and Bruno manned the quad .50, while Spec. 6 Freddie Fillers, the chief cook, commandeered an M-60 machine gun. Between the two weapons, the trio let loose hundreds of rounds. At least three more sappers were cut down trying to make their way to safety.

A Night Hawk Huey gunship, with a starlight scope aboard, was the first aircraft on the scene. The chopper, flown by Capt. Norman Hayes, was from Trp. D, 1st Sqdn., 1st Cal. Hayes had to fly his helicopter at a higher altitude due to the thick smoke coming from the burning hootches at Mary Ann.

But the gunship did score some kills. "[We] ... could actually see the VC in the wire... It looked like they were trying to take people out of the wire... We engaged, and I know that anything we fired on ceased firing at us," said Hayes.

In the end, however, only 15 VC bodies were found. Evidence indicated the enemy dug a few hasty graves to bury their dead before withdrawing.

Unfortunately, by the time reinforcements arrived, the assault was over. It had lasted just an hour. The results were disastrous: 30 GIs killed and 82 wounded.

C Company was hardest hit, with 20 KIA alone. The Battery C platoon sustained five KIA, 25% of its men.

(Incidentally, website claims that some of the deaths were due to "friendly fire" are absolutely wrong.)

Maj. Gen. James L. Baldwin, commanding general of the Americal Division, arrived on the scene at dawn.

"The firebase was a shambles", he wrote in a letter home, "with things burning all over the place... There were many [soldiers] who were sitting around with rather dazed looks on their faces, and another group which was actively and energetically trying to pick up the pieces. There were no in-betweens."

Intelligence & Negligence

The consequences of the attack were quickly felt. In the aftermath of an investigation, Baldwin and Col. William S. Hathaway, the 196th LIB commander, were relieved of duty. Both would retired soon afterward. A host of other officers were reprimanded, including the hard-driving Lt. Col. Doyle. He remained in the service until his retirement, but never received another promotion.

Many felt Baldwin's reprimand unjust. "It was a political thing," said Capt. John Strand, commanding officer (CO) of A Co., 1st Bn., 46th Inf. "Scapegoats were needed... What happened to Baldwin was wrong, but it's not hard for me to understand given how big organizations work."

Spec. 4 Ed Newton also felt "It was not right what they did to Baldwin. Hell, he was the division commander. It was a brigade and battalion problem. The day before we got hit they had us pull in all the sensors from around the perimeter.

This is an important fact, as I reviewed this article. I knew about perimeter security, especially around fire support bases. I couldn't understand how the VC penetrated what should have been a fortified perimeter; with razor wire stacked 3 and 4 coils high, claymore mines, trip flares, grenades, and many surprises that should have been out there. But they ordered these items remove, thus the onslaught was made possible. The bunker guards were not high or sleeping, they were relying on perimeter security, and nothing was there.

"Kim, our Kit Carson Scout, warned us we were infiltrated. He said the enemy was posing as ARVNs on the base. One ARVN officer even inquired about the easiest way to get off the firebase to fish.

"We thought that was strange and nobody told him. In fact, the night of the attack, we took fire from the ARVN position. When we returned fire, it stopped. Not one ARVN came out to help us. And the enemy left them alone.

"We tried to tell the officers what Kim had said, but they didn't listen to us. It was poor intelligence and gross negligence---plain and simple."

Allegations of drug use also have hovered over the performance of the GIs at Mary Ann.

Platoon Sgt. Bill Walker, who was in charge of bunkers 15 through 22, has a different viewpoint:

"Everyone was awake when I made my rounds. There was no pot in my bunkers. And I know what pot smells like. One soldier, manning a bunker by the trash dump, was dozing. I stayed with him for a few minutes to make sure he was awake, then I returned to my bunker. Not two minutes later, everything hit the fan."

Sgt. Gary L. Noller, a battalion radio operator for the 46th Infantry, recalled: "The belief that the enemy would not waste its time attacking a force that was soon leaving anyway led to a false sense of security. And while drugs were present on Mary Ann, they were used only by a minority of soldiers."

For several years Mary Ann had been a non-threatening fire base, and the lack of disciple and poor attitudes had become commonplace. There were allegations of drug use and lack luster security the months prior to the attack. The war was growing old, the reports from back home were discouraging, the mission in Vietnam was vague. Excuses; no reality.

There were reports, made by ARVN (Army of the Republic of South Vietnam) "Kit Carson Scouts" that the fire base had been infiltrated by VC who pretended to be ARVN soldiers. These reports were basically ignored by command. The night before the attack Mary Ann took fire from an ARVN position outside the perimeter. When fire was returned, everything stopped. Not one ARVN on the base came out to help. These incidences were reported to command, and again were ignored. In my opinion, we had very little input as grunts/draftees; the lifers didn't really care about our information. After all, we were all expendable, that's why we were there.

Why Mary Ann?

Why had the enemy made such a determined effort to overrun Mary Ann? It was late in the war, and Vietnamization was progressing steadily. GIs were being replaced by ARVN units.

Timothy Baldwin, son of Gen. Baldwin, who did extensive research on Mary Ann to clear his deceased father's name, may have found the answer:

"The 1/46th was causing too much trouble from... Mary Ann."

Just two weeks before the assault, the unit had unearthed a large enemy cache. Sgt. 1st Class Edward "Pop" Manson, platoon sergeant of the 4.2–inch mortar platoon, agrees: "Charlie was after Company C... they got the CO [Knight] in his bunker, too..."

Baldwin interviewed several Mary Ann VC veterans: they had no idea the Americans were about to abandon the firebase and turn it over to ARVN. "The VC," Baldwin wrote, "normally known for their superb intelligence-gathering, had failed on this issue."

That American courage was displayed on Mary Ann is indisputable. Silver Stars were awarded to Sgt. Elmer R. Head, Capt. Virtus A. Savage, senior medic Larry J. Vogelsang (a conscientious objector), Sgt. Ervin E. Powell, 1st Lt. Jerry W. Sams, Pfc. Paul G. Grooms, 1st Lt. Arthur D. Schmidt, Capt. Paul Spilberg and Spec 4 David Tarnay.

In one legendary exploit, 1st Lt. C. Barry McGee choked a sapper to death before being killed.

Recognizing Hardships

In Sappers In The Wire: The Life And Death of Firebase Mary Ann (1995), the late author Keith W. Nolan counters many bogus claims. "Unfortunately, we historians got it wrong," he wrote.

"I do not mean to whitewash what happened at Firebase Mary Ann with such a remark, for the incident was a tragic disaster with much to teach today's soldiers about vigilance.

"What I do mean to say is that commentary which tars the 1/46th Infantry as a 'mob'... is grossly exaggerated. Most of the draftees on Mary Ann had already proven themselves in combat. And yet, however reluctantly, there were still soldiers like those in the 1/46th Infantry out fighting the war. There hardships should be recognized.

"Author [Geoffrey] Perret got it right when he wrote that these troops who 'had faith in nothing much, least of all in men like Johnson and Nixon,' still 'served their country a lot better than it served them.'"

I tell this story to illustrate some of the bullshit we, as Vietnam Vets, had to endure for the love and respect of our country. The above story is not my own words, but a reprint of an article I read in the March 2011 VFW magazine. The author of the article, Al Hemmingway, is a member of VFW Post 201 in Waterbury, Ct. I also appreciate the contributions from Timothy Baldwin. He did extensive research that otherwise would not have been done to clear his father's reputation. Major Gen. James L. Baldwin, commanding general of the Americal Division, was relieved of his command and retired.

I fought side by side with guys who were in country and attached to 1/46th Company B when this tragedy occurred, they never mentioned it. I knew something had gone wrong on Mary Ann, but I never pressed the matter. It was for those there, unspoken.

I suspect my Company rotated in and out of Mary Ann as part of their duties. I did find out recently that B Company was several clicks (kilometers) from Mary Ann and they had to watch helplessly as the firebase was attacked. Our Company Clerk, Mike Post, had just gotten in country and was out on his 1st or 2nd mission when the firebase was over run. According to his eyewitness account of the attack, it lasted for quite a while and lit up the entire AO. It was night time and they could not immediately move. A few days after the attack, B Company provided security on Mary Ann.

I know that Company C was a fighting force to be reckoned with; I saw them in action several times out in the bush.

Reprinted with permission. March 2011, VFW Magazine.

To include this reprint I needed to get permission from the author, Al Hemingway, I wrote him a letter requesting the use of his article. After a week or so I received a nice note from Mr. Hemingway; **"It's indeed an honor to be quoted in your book–Welcome Home Brother!!!!"**

That note means a lot to me.

Chapter 6

"Move out," Sgt. Steele barked. We were leaving the relative comfort of the chopper pad. Our re-supply complete, it was time to move out. It was getting late and we'd be setting up our NDP soon. We climbed up a steep trail toward the firebase. I assumed that we would spend the night there.

It took about 40 minutes to make our way up to Fire Support Base Linda. This was my first encounter with an artillery unit. In my opinion they were sitting ducks, whereas us grunts were always on the move. A moving target is harder to hit. I'd soon find out why we were there.

We came to a clearing where we could assemble and receive our instructions. Steele assigned two men to a bunker. These bunkers were well fortified with three sides enclosed with sandbags. The front was open to allow the guards to see forward. The corrugated tin roof was covered with three layers of sandbags. The bunkers were dark and damp, with a folding cot in the back corner. Steele assigned Pogo and I to the same bunker. Pogo had been here before and said this will be a nice break from the shit. He explained that we would be here for three or four days to provide extra security for the firebase. There was Intel, the firebase might be attacked within 24 to 48 hours.

Pogo wasn't too upset about this. "Firebases are difficult for the VC to overrun, and now they know we are here in force," he said. "What we'll do is take two-hour shifts tonight. We'll catch some Z's in between our shifts. So let's get settled, I'm gettin' fuckin' hungry."

Pogo and I had concocted a combination of c-rats, a LRPP (long range patrol packet) and hot sauce which he swiped from the mess hall. He told me that some guys were good at doctoring up this shit we have to eat. As we ate and talked, I got to know Pogo. Up to now he had just been a guy helping me along, but now we were rapping and joking with each other like friends. This was my first chance to relax in Vietnam; it had been a busy first few days out in the bush!

I didn't get much sleep that first night. Guard duty was boring, and it was difficult to stay awake for two hours at a time. We had no night sighting devices; we had to rely on our own site and hearing. The perimeter outside the bunkers was well fortified. Razor wire,

Claymore mines, trip flares and other surprises were all over the place. They were always there day and night.

For breakfast we could eat at the small makeshift mess hut here on the hill. Pogo went first and was gone for about 45 minutes. He told me he got talking to Steele and a few of the other guys. He said the food was okay and at least we didn't have to eat out of cans. I made my way to the small shack with a sign "Mess" marked on it. After chowin' down I returned to the bunker, and we pulled guard duty for the rest of the day. I was able to relax and catch a few Z's that afternoon.

By the third day this was "getting old", as we would say. I got to know Pogo better. We talked about the ambush and he told me that a guy who got injured was a friend of his. He told me losing friends was to be expected in Nam.

"What happened to him?" I asked.

"Don't know," Pogo replied. "Don't mean nothin'." Then silence.

I wanted to thank him for helping me, but after that exchange, I kept quiet. He was seasoned, and he knew what he was doing. I could only hope to be as prepared.

The next morning, we left the firebase and made our way back down to the helicopter pad to catch our choppers back to the rear. They call this "stand down" which meant we would get cleaned up, get medical attention if needed, have a few hot meals, lots of luke warm showers and a bed to sleep on, at least for a few days.

The chopper ride back to the rear was exciting and exhilarating; I was leaving the bush and heading to a more normal place. I wasn't sure what I would do once I got back, I'd follow everyone else's lead, and do what they did. The choppers set down on the LZ one at a time, dropping off 6 to 8 of us. We made our way back to the Company area, and turned in our M-16s, grenades, flares, Claymore mines and ammo to the armory. The Armory Sgt. checked our name off his list to confirm that all munitions and weapons had been turned in. When he got to me, he growled,

"Name," he did not recognize me.

"Freeborn," I shot back.

"You're not on my list," he replied.

"I'm new in the unit; I went out in a hurry a few days ago," I explained.

"All right spell it." He wrote my name on his clipboard and took all my stuff.

"Will I get the same M-16 back?" I asked.

"Na, they're all the same, next," he continued.

I made my way back to the single-story hootches I had occupied a few days earlier. I dropped my ruck on an empty bunk, where I found a pillow and a blanket and a used soiled mattress. I improvised and used my field bedding to get settled in. On my way to the hootch I passed the outdoor showers. I needed to get cleaned up, so I grabbed a towel, soap and headed to the showers. A line had formed; I was fifth or sixth in line for the three available showers. The showers were nothing more than tanks of water gravity-fed through a hose with a shower head attached. The water, warm from sitting in the sun, felt good as it washed over me. I finished up, wrapped my towel around me and returned to my bunk.

Later, laying there looking up at the words "Arnold Ziffel" painted on the roof, I wondering what was to become of me, here in Nam. It was the first time I had a free moment to think of all that had happened. The hootch was quiet as I lay there contemplating my fate when a few guys came in.

"Hey Freeborn what the hell ya doing?"

"Nothing much," I replied.

"We're going over to the EM club, do ya want to come?" someone asked.

"Sure, let me get my stuff put away, I'll be right there."

So much for pondering life in Vietnam, it was time to get busy living it.

The EM club, a make-shift bar with a pool table and jukebox, was crowded. Our Company filled the club with guys I had only seen and not met. I felt out of place, like a stranger at a local neighborhood bar. There were tables and chairs and a small stage. Everyone was talking, laughing and having a good time. I sat there with Hud, Pogo and a couple other guys. The beer was cold, and the conversation was interesting. This being the first evening back in the rear, everyone was kicking back after this dangerous mission. I had only been out there for a few days, they had completed almost 3 weeks in the bush.

After a while I returned to the hootch looking forward to a good night's sleep. The place was quiet; a few guys were playing cards and BS-ing. It was about 8:30 PM, I thought I'd write a few letters, I wanted to get them in tomorrow's mail.

The next few days in the rear, I got to know the guys in my squad. In Nam being part of a squad was like being part of a family, and the seasoned grunts showed that closeness. I was unknown to them and would have to prove myself by keeping my shit together and going along with the program.

I got to know Hudson and Pogo out in the bush. They seemed willing to accept me as a squad member, we became familiar with each other and they seemed okay with me.

My squad leader, Sgt. Steele was "short", which meant he only had a few weeks to go in country. During this stand down Festus (Ken Freeman) told us he was taking over for Steele. Festus was a shake and bake, meaning he went to NCO (Non-Commissioned Officer) school. I hadn't met Festus, but I'd seen him out in the bush.

Then there was Doc Shaw, our squad's medic. Doc, a conscientious objector, did not carry an M-16 but he did pack a 45 caliber pistol. Nice guy, easy to approach and always upbeat.

Pudgy, our point man, and Reese were always together. I had given Pudgy a pound cake my first day in the bush. We spoke a few times after that and became friends.

Ed Stanke from Wisconson, and Ron Jankowski from Pennslyvania came in the company with me. They were assigned to different squads, but we became fast friends.

Three days into stand down my squad would take on a complete personnel change. Festus, our new squad leader, informed us that some new guys would join our squad. It was early September when the newbies arrived. Terry Barbe, Bob Hampel, Carl Whittenbach, Don Proctor, Fitzroy Pringle, Dan Gerleve, Mike Detzi and Arthur Abbott would join the squad. For all they knew, I'd been in country for months.

The next two days we got ready to go back out to the bush, the squad shaped up as follows:

Terry Barbe, our new pig gunner, stood about 6'2" with broad shoulders and a muscular athletic build; a perfect choice to hump the gun.

Bob Hampel would be assistant pig gunner.

Dan Gerleve humped the radio.

Doc continued as our medic.

Speed (Carl Whittenbach), Proctor (Don Proctor) and Diz (Mike Detzi) would be riflemen as would Pringle (Fitzroy Pringle) and Tennessee (Arthur Abbott).

I volunteered to carry the M-203 grenade launcher. At the time, the grenade launcher was a classified weapon. There were no public pictures or descriptions of this weapon. Stateside I trained on an older version, the M-79. The M-203 was an M-16 with a grenade launcher mounted under the barrel. I wore a vest containing thirty, 40 mm grenades. They looked like large bullets. This was our new squad; Pogo and Hudson were assigned to CP (Command Post) as was Pudgy and Reese.

Our LT, (Lieutenant, platoon leader) injured on the last mission, would not be returning to the bush. He was sent to Germany to recover from the shrapnel wounds he received during the ambush a few weeks earlier. We would go out on our next mission with our Company Commander, Capt. Mac. I was told that Capt. Mac was a real pain in the ass. He was very demanding and would go out of his way to make life more miserable than it already was. My brief experience out in the bush had not prepared me for what would come. Capt. Mac would be everything the guys told me, and more. He was gung-ho and always on us, pushing us during that next mission.

Chapter 7

September 9, 1971

Hi Joey,

We still haven't heard from the last letter but I've given your address to everyone and I hope you have been getting some mail.

Sister Mary Margaret promised to write and I'm sure she will be of some help to you, she really is a good woman.

Everything here is okay, and the car will be taken care of. All we are doing is going to work, etc. but I'll try to write every week, or more if I can. We still want to know what you can use and you'll have it.

I hope it hasn't been too hot for you over there, and from what we hear the action has been quiet. Make the best of what is going on and stay clear of all the Vietnamese.

Tom went back to school today, and he seems to like the high school better than the other one.

I'll write often but the letters won't be too long, the main thing is to get something to you. How long these take to get to you we have no way of knowing, so the more we can keep them coming to you the better.

Jeff has been over a couple of times, he's selling the store, and now has a job in Middletown and is doing okay. He got his new draft card and is now classified 1A so he will be eligible if his number comes up.

Take good care of yourself and don't take too many chances. Eat all you can get but stay away from the local food.

Will write again in a few days.

Love, Dad.

I got this letter while out in the bush. I had a water tight ammo box, and I kept all my letters, to re-read when I needed to. The letters my father wrote were very meaningful and I would often sense his mood, anxiety level and hopefulness.

September 8, 1971

Dear Sis,

Hi, how are you? I haven't heard from you as yet, so I decided to write you. If you haven't written me yet, I'd advise you to do so promptly, okay? I would sure like hearing from you.

Well, there isn't much happening at the present. The company is sort of "shamming" that is goofing off. All we do is pull security on a mortar hill. In a few days however we'll be going out in the bush for 16 days or so. I wanted to write you sooner and give you an idea of things I'll need these next rainy months ahead. Right now the weather is beautiful so I'm not concerned. However by the end of this month, we will be in the midst of the Monsoon Season. So it will be important to have a lot of hot food and drinks during this time. The Army supplies a limited quantity of such items. If you sent me a package, it would make life a lot more pleasant and healthier for me. I could use: instant, dried soup, (for instance-Lipton) the kind that is in packets, all you do is add hot water. (A few broth cubes) also iced tea mix, with lemon, five or six packets. One can of sterno (heating gel) and Sis, if you can find them, a few good types of space food sticks. I heard they are very good. You could also think of something else, edible that might be of some help. Anything you send will be very welcomed. Don't hurry the package, however. Try to get it to me by the end of September okay?

Well Sis, I guess I'll end here. I hope you can write me soon. I'll anxiously wait to hear from you. Take care of yourself and give my best to everyone.

Love, Joey

I wanted to get this letter to my sister Suzanne; she was 22, out of school and working for Texaco Research Labs in Beacon, NY. She liked to travel with her girlfriends, and life was going well for her.

I hoped she could find these and other useful items as the rainy season was coming; I thought I'd better be prepared.

September 11, 1971

Hi Joey,

I'm sending a letter from Sister Mary, she says she sent it to you but it was returned, why I don't know?

We are all okay here and I had the car going tonight up and down the road and it seems to be in perfect shape, but it does need to be run now and then.

Write to Sister her address is Sister Mary Margaret, Mount St. Mary's Infirmary, Newburgh, New York 12550. Take care I'll write again soon we miss you.

Love, Dad

I read the nice letter from Sr. Mary Margaret, and it came to me at a good time, I needed some prayers and to read the things she wrote.

She said she would remember me in her daily prayers. She told me the prayer she would pray each morning:

"Dear Jesus, I accept whatever sufferings you send me today for the grace of a happy death and in reparation for the sins of my past life. I also say an Act of Contrition each morning and evening. Then if our Lord chooses to have me die that day or night, I will have told Him I am sorry for my sins."

She reminded me that she had shared a room at St. Luke's Hospital with my mother and she went on to tell me she loved her. She told me about her nephew who was in Vietnam for a couple of years. He was assigned to a postal division, and didn't see combat. She asked me to pray for her as well, and for me to offer up my fears and anxiety for her and my family, and to write her again if I got the chance.

This letter was quite uplifting, and I felt her prayers each day. It was good that someone was praying for me, and I would keep this elderly retired Sister in my prayers. She was helpful to my mother in her time of need, now she would help me.

September 14, 1971

Dear Sis,

Hi, how are you? I am fine. I received your letter today and was very pleased to hear from you. I usually reply to letters with the one sent available, so I'm sure I'll answer any questions that might be asked. Well, at present I don't have yours handy, it's tucked on the bottom of my rucksack. I'll try to remember what you wrote okay? I read the letter twice, so it shouldn't be too hard.

Well, I often thought about your trip (Puerto Rico), I regret I couldn't stick around until you got home to tell us all about it. I guess it was really nice, and I would have enjoyed seeing the pictures. I agree with what you said about how another country and its people can change your outlook on things. Here in Vietnam, you see the peasant population nearly every day. They work the rice paddies and what not, a lot of the women work as hootch maids. They keep the living areas clean for the GI's. I wouldn't know about that too much, but when I'm in the rear, I'm in contact with the Vietnamese a lot. I used to think these people were backward savages, but now that I am understanding their customs and ways, my opinion has changed. Being here also makes me appreciate many of the things I had back in the world. Such things as a bed, a blanket, a cold drink and things like that. Many of the necessities in the states are luxuries to the Vietnamese, and some would be luxuries to me also. I imagine I'll mature a lot while I'm over here.

I was shocked to hear Jeff is 1A. I sure hope he doesn't get drafted. I think it would be impossible for the US Army to indoctrinate our brother Jeff. Tell him the next time you see him to leave the country if necessary. Mexico or South America, it's not worth killing yourself by going into the Army. I know what it's all about. It might sound as if I was unpatriotic, but I'm not. I'm against this war and against killing anything that has life. If I had it to do over again, I wouldn't be in Vietnam.

You sure got a good deal on that tape player. For the cost of two speakers, you can't go wrong. This tape player is a good make also (Panasonic). I'm planning to order one and send it home. I'm not sure when I'll be doing it however, all the walking I do sure keeps me busy. We'll be in the rear in five more days so I might be able to do something then. I also bought a cassette tape player. It's just a cheap one, but it's all right. I can't buy any tapes for it however, they don't sell cassette tapes in this country. If you should see any prerecorded tapes such as Grand Funk Railroad either "Grand Funk Live", or "Closer to Home", I would sure dig receiving them in the mail. I'll be glad to pay you back the money, for they are expensive. So if you should happen to see them get them, okay? Remember either one, not both and look for Three Dog Night.

Well, I guess I'll end here. I mailed a letter with some things I could use, included. I would appreciate anything sent. Well Sis, take care of yourself, give my best to everyone and write me again soon!

Love, Joey

September 19, 1971

Dear Dad,

How are you? I am fine. I received a letter from you the other day, with a letter from Sister (Sr. Mary Margaret) enclosed. I have already written her, and I'll be sending it off later today when the resupply bird comes in. Right now

I've just eaten breakfast and awaiting word to move out. We have been working in the low lands as of late, looking for "dinks". We haven't been too successful however, booby-traps have taken two lives already and injured five others. Don't be alarmed by this because that's what's happening over here. You seldom see the enemy but you know he has been around. The casualties were the first for the company in about a year. We were all shaken by the events and we had yesterday off. Today's another work day however, and I pray all will go well.

I'm glad the car is running good. It's a good car and with a little work, I can make it better. I'm glad I didn't sell it. Money to pay for it is available. I'll have no trouble keeping the payments up. I guess I'll be getting my Spec/4 rank in the near future and that means over $300 a month. With my MOS (Military Occupational Specialty) I don't spend too much money. I'm glad for that.

Well, I guess I'll get this letter off now. Take good care of yourself and give my best to everyone at home. Write me soon.

Love, Joey

I wrote this letter after a very bad day while we were performing a human sweep of an area that reportedly contained a large cache of enemy munitions and supplies. As we walked abreast in formation, we could see and hear explosive devices detonating; Bouncing Betties mostly and some toe poppers and other nasty booby-traps. Every step could have been our last, yet we continued to move forward, as ordered. I was really scared, and visual detection of these explosive devices was nearly impossible. Finally, the command came to hold in place; too many men were getting killed or injured. I froze, and we carefully made our way back to a safer area, they aborted the mission and called in gunships.

Below I remember the two men who died that day.

PFC. Larry Ehler, Algonquin, IL

11B10 Infantry—Age 19

Start Tour Date: 08/27/1971

Incident Date: 09/17/1971

Casualty Date: 09/17/1971

Location: Quang Nam Province

Wall Panel—WS Line 19

PFC. Miguel Bynoe – Jamaica, NY

11B10 Infantry—Age 22

Start Tour Date: 08/27/1971

Incident Date: 09/17/1971

Casualty Date: 09/17/1971

Location: Quang Nam Province

Wall Panel—WS Line 19

September 22, 1971

Hi Joey,

Just a short note to let you know we got two letters today one dated the 12th and the 15th. I'm glad to hear you're doing the best you can. Don't give up, I know these times are not the best but we have got to go through them somehow. There's a saying that goes:

" Smile–Anyhow".

I think you're right about getting out of the thick of things. I will write to Fish (Congressman Hamilton Fish Jr.) tonight and try to get through the idea that you could be useful somewhere else. It's not easy what you're doing and I'm sure most people don't even realize what this whole thing is all about. Keep your courage, even when things don't go right, this one thing is the hardest to do, but you will be better for it. You're homesick now and we miss you just as much, but feel that where you are now has to be done and enter into it to the best of your ability. When I had to do KP, I pretended I was a cook, this made me able to get through it. I hope you know what I mean. We are sending you a couple of packages, of things you wanted and will keep up the flow, they will be small, we hope enough of them will reach you. If there is something else you need let us know.

Angela called and told me you sent a picture to her and that we could expect one too.

Try to conserve your strength, which I know is sometimes impossible but if you do feel bad, don't be afraid to ask for medical attention. Take care and we miss you.

Love, Dad

This letter is my Dad's response to a letter I wrote, I was feeling really down and the tone of the letter was negative. My father always helped me keep things in perspective though. He refers to contacting our Congressman Hamilton Fish Jr. and I did get a Congressional Inquiry later in my tour.

September 28, 1971

Dear Dad,

I received your letter dated September 22, and it was good hearing from you. I also received Suzanne's letter this morning as well. Well I guess you received the letter I wrote almost 20 days ago, about how I felt. You should have received my next letter, before this one reaches you. I was feeling poorly when I wrote the letter. I was upset, and perhaps over emotional. I don't know. I just get so uptight about being over here. I still don't want to do what I'm here to do. My health has improved, and now, as I write this letter, I'm in excellent shape. As long as I'm physically well, I'll keep my head together, when I start breaking down, everything goes. I didn't complain to anyone when I was feeling sick, this time. In the event I should ever become unstable or weak again, I will give it to someone, and let them worry about it. If I'm to endure the life of "grunt", I must stay healthy and I'm convinced of this. Don't worry about me. I've got strength through our Lord, and that's all that really matters. I pray for you all and ask for your prayers also.

Well, I've heard from Angie, she wrote and told me she contacted you when she returned home. Her trip was nice, and she enjoyed herself very much. She also mentioned visiting you soon. Perhaps she has already. It makes me feel good that she thinks so fondly of you, and I hope she visits often.

I had a picture taken of me, it's on the way. You don't have any of me since I've been in the Army, so this will be it. It's a nice picture, I hope you like it.

Well Dad, I'll write you again soon, and don't worry about me. I'll be fine. Take care of yourself. Give my best to everyone. How is Tom? I've got to write him one of these days, take care. Love, Joey

I was uneasy about the previous letter, I didn't want my Dad to worry about me and I didn't want to complain. Most times I wrote upbeat letters. I got good at deception because the truth about this place was hard for anyone to take. This war affected more people than those who served here.

September 30, 1971

Hi Joey,

We've gotten a few letters from you and were glad to hear that you're at a base now, at least you have a few comforts. I also got the check, but don't worry about the car. I'll put the money in an account for you.

I sent a couple of packages last week. I hope they reached you before this. I'll keep on sending them often, small packages; I think will be easier to handle and may reach you sooner.

This is Thurs night, and we just got home, so I just wanted to get this off to let you know all is okay. Angie told me about the picture but we still haven't gotten it, I'll keep looking.

The weather has still been rainy but we do get a good day now and then, yesterday was one of them.

I'm sending a package of tapes from Suzanne, I'll get it off tomorrow, she said you asked for them.

Let us know how the packages reach you and whatever else you want just holler and it'll be on the way.

Pauline (my aunt) should be writing quite a bit to you, we are going to Christine's wedding sometime in November. It's on a Sunday, so we will probably leave on Friday night and come back on Sunday. She wants us to stay until Thanksgiving but we can't get that much time off. I'll be lucky to get Saturday off. I'll say so long for now and will write again soon. Take care of yourself.

Love, Dad

This was a short, late night letter my Dad wrote, after working from 9:00 AM to 9:00 PM at the shoe store. By Thursday night he was tired. Retail in those days were 6 days a week. Sunday was his only day to get chores done and run errands for the family.

He didn't like weddings too much, but I could sense he was looking forward to this one. My Aunt Pauline wrote my Dad often. She would write me also, and I always enjoyed her writing style and her news and stories from Long Island.

The picture I sent home never arrived, but Angie's did. It's the only copy I have. Later in my tour I had another picture taken to replace the one that got lost. I liked the first one better.

Chapter 8

Our next mission included the lowlands, located slightly northwest of Da Nang, a rugged area with lots of rice paddies and some elevated terrain. Our mission was to sweep an area looking for a cache of weapons and munitions the enemy had stored away for future offensives. The lowlands consisting of small villages, no infrastructure like roads, running water, etc. These vills, as we called them, were out on their own, vulnerable to VC infiltration. Many times the VC used these civilian villages to hide their weapons and munitions from us. In 1971, the war for U.S. Forces had become a defensive operation. We could no longer be aggressive or offensive. The rules of engagement had changed; fire only if fired on first was the official decree. For us going into vills was political, too many bad things had happened in vills visited by our military. The Government was trying diplomacy as a new approach to winning hearts and minds.

Off in a distance I noticed choppers in formation heading our way. They set down, and we boarded them by squad. The sliding side doors were open; the passenger compartment was large enough to accommodate one squad. They brought in 6 choppers so we would have fewer men in each chopper. I climbed in and sat on the edge of the open side door, legs dangling out. I had seen other guys doing this, so I decided I'd try it. My last trip on a chopper I hung on for dear life. Now, with nothing to hold on to, I sat there looking straight ahead. I could see the other choppers flying alongside ours, observing legs dangling, door gunners at the ready, and a lot of quiet anxiety. No one knew what to expect; we had to be ready for anything.

The choppers descended, one at a time, checking for small arms fire upon approach. The pilots were chattering to each other as our chopper hovered over the reed grass; we jumped out. There was no enemy fire, the LZ was secure. We immediately went to the perimeter of the LZ and set up OP (observation post) for security of the remaining choppers. Before long, we were making our way to a wooded area to re-group and move out.

We humped for several hours that day; eventually making our way to the NDP (nighttime defensive position). We did the usual setup routine, only this time the new guys were asking me things. I did the best I could to help them along, at least the ones near me. I had Speed and Bull on either side of me. I helped them with their perimeter security; after all it was my security as well. I was glad to help, and to know where everything was located. I paid particular attention to the M-18 Claymore mine setup, making sure they were capped correctly and facing in the right direction, away from us and toward the enemy. I checked out the clackers and reminded the newbies how they worked. If we needed to fire them, we were all in a "world of hurt", hit the clacker 3 times and hope for the best.

These Claymore mines contained a full pound of C4, with plates of steel-beaded balls laminated within the heavy plastic curved housing. The VC had a bad habit of turning these Claymores around, facing us, and then if we fired them off they'd rain down shit on us. To prevent this, we carefully connected a trip flare, with a hair trigger. If someone tampered with the Claymore, the flair would go off. The newbies knew this; they were well trained, I just felt better reminding them.

The monsoon season was beginning; the weather was getting damp and cool. It rained more frequently now, and soon would be raining day and night. Talking to the older grunts during our recent stand down, I got some useful information about NDP bedding set up. The hammock we carried was to keep us off the ground, especially during the rainy season. We tied our water proof poncho between two trees in a tent-like configuration, about 6 feet off the ground. Then about 5 feet off the ground we'd string our hammocks. Then stuff our inflated air mattress inside the hammock. This kept us off the ground and out of the relentless rain. The lightweight poncho liner blanket kept us warm. This was comfortable and better than sleeping on the ground. It took practice to setup this way and sometimes the terrain would not allow it. More than once, I slept on the ground with just my poncho over me.

The mission was uneventful; we patrolled a large area, mostly marsh and reed grass. There were a few slow-moving streams we had to cross, sometimes waist high. When leeches got on us, we used lit cigarettes or "bug juice" (insect repellent) to remove them. Even with tightly bloused pant legs, they'd latch on and suck blood until removed. We were discouraged from scraping them off with a knife or bayonet, as that would only remove the leech body. The suckers stayed attached and could cause bleeding and infection. Bug juice worked the best. This was definitely a leech-infested mission, and we all complained about them.

In the bush, they re-supplied us every 3 or 4 days. We always needed dry clothes and socks. Skin fungus, aka Jungle Rot, was a result of being wet all the time. Wet feet, if left unattended, could be a problem for us also, causing our feet to hurt, making humping that more difficult. Keeping dry was a challenge.

During the rainy season however, staying dry was impossible. I learned that I could function just as well soaking wet, as I could on a dry sunny day. This was called getting acclimated to your environment. Nothing could prevent us from accomplishing the mission.

Our re-supply was to happen later in the afternoon on the third day out. The weather was temporarily improving, cloud cover was high and the brightness of the sun made it ideal. It took a few hours to carved out an LZ for the re-supply chopper. Basically, we would have an easy day as the re-supply took precedence, at least as far as we were concerned.

Maybe I'd get mail; I could use a letter from home. I'd have to wait'n see!

Chapter 9

We were back, but everything had changed. They had moved us to a new rear area called Freedom Hill. The new base was closer to the PX and other services we needed when in the rear. This had been a Marine base, and because of the new unit change from the 23rd infantry, they re-purposed it for the 196th Light Infantry Brigade.

I liked this new area; it had two-story barracks, with bathrooms, showers and hot running water. We had bunk beds and lots of common areas where we assembled, played cards, hung out. We also had a real EM (enlisted men's) club. They would have shows and we'd spend a lot of time there when in the rear.

Our stand down was over, three days was all we had to decompress, it was time to make our way down to the chopper pad. There was lots of activity as we loaded up our ruck sack, stuffing them with whatever we could get our hands on. It was again go time, and this mission would probably be wet. Monsoon season was upon us and it was getting cooler.

Birds-in-bound, someone yelled! We strapped on our rucks and made our way to the incoming choppers. Here we go again!

It was now raining every day, all day. We were patrolling the lowlands northwest of Da Nang to prepare for the fireworks the VC would send to Da Nang on Election Day. It seemed the VC pulled out all the stops on the South Vietnamese free elections; they would launch mortars and rockets towards the airbase and civilian targets, with impunity. Human life was meaningless to them; these attacks were evidence of that. The civilian population and military personnel were well prepared for these attacks. They had bunkers constructed everywhere, and when the sirens sounded, everyone would head for these fortifications.

October 2, 1971, another rainy morning; I had just dried out from the day before. In the evening I removed my wet clothing and hung them under my make-shift tent. In the morning I would dress using these damp clothes, only to get soaked again within minutes. Once I got used to being wet, it became second nature, and almost unnoticeable. We had to go about our mission wet or dry; that's the way we lived during the monsoons.

The fire ball startled me as the rocket launched from a wooded area just below my night time defensive position.

"What the hell was that?" I yelled.

"Rockets," someone shouted back.

We immediately went into our defensive posture, as if being attacked. The VC had set up a timed launch of several rockets, aimed crudely towards Da Nang. They probably detonated somewhere other than their intended target, but they were disruptive, just the same. It was Election Day, and hence, the rocket attack. I was only a few meters from the launch site, and it was too close for comfort. We spent the rest of that day patrolling the area, finding only remnants that Charlie had been there.

The mission had been extended due to Election Day. Things had settled down and we were going back to base in a few days, but we needed a re-supply before then. I wrote some letters so I could get them mailed out. I really had to plan my letter writing because I couldn't just drop the letters in a mailbox. I had to wait for the re-supply and plan accordingly.

I had fallen behind in my letter writing, and this extended mission gave me plenty of time to catch up. We did a lot of letter writing out in the bush; it was a quiet thing to do. For obvious reasons unnecessary noise and chatter was discouraged out there.

October 2, 1971

Dear Dad,

Hi, how are you? I'm doing fine. Well, right now I'm back out in the bush. I just cleaned my M-16 and my ammo and am left with nothing more to do. So I decided to write.

I got paid the other day and my voucher was short $100, because the financial people got me mixed up with someone else and their $100 support allotment. I'm supposed to get reimbursed next month. I won't be able to send any money home this month, or next month. I'll make up for it. I'm thinking of increasing my bond to $50. I will use the money for the loan I have.

The mission I'm on now is supposed to last 17 days. It may be extended however with the election and all; they seem to think a long mission is worthwhile. We go in on stand down after this mission, so there's something to look forward to. Did you send that letter to Fish? It sounded real good and that might be just what I need to get out of the bush.

Well Dad, it looks like rain, so I'll say goodbye. Take care of yourself and give my best to all.

Love Joey,

PS. The picture will be home soon.

October 4, 1971

Hi Joey,

Suzanne and I both got a letter from you today and you certainly sound a lot better, sure glad you feel a little stronger, but there are times when all of us are tired and nothing looks good.

Keep your faith in God and I'm sure all will be okay. I pray for you every day that you are over there. Sr. Mary Margaret also has you in her prayers, so how can you lose. I can't say how much we miss you, take care of yourself and will try to do the same here; of course, it's much easier here. Have courage Joey our thoughts are always with you.

I was hoping you would have gotten one of the parcels but evidently you haven't. I hope you can use what is in them.

I'll get this off to you now and will try to get Tom to write you, but if you can send him a letter.

Take care Joey and I'll write again soon.

Love Dad

October 7, 1971

Hi Joe,

It's been a while since I've had a minute to sit down and get a note off to you, so here I am. How is it going by this time? In your last couple of letters you made its sound half–way decent; at least temporarily.

Not too much has been happening around here lately. We're all looking forward to Christine's wedding in a few weeks, six I think. I'm supposed to go to another wedding that day, but I will not be able to. I guess we'll go down to Long Island on Friday night and returned on Sunday morning. It should be a nice weekend.

By this time you must have gotten the small package I sent you. Now did you like the tapes? I thought they were good, but then our taste in music might be different. In any case I hope you enjoy them.

I have bad news, Lucky (our dog) died on Monday. Mr. Pendolino called us and said Lucky was laying down on his property crying, and didn't look like he could move, so we didn't move him, by the next day he was gone. I think you know he had the mange all summer and at one point I made an appointment to have him put to sleep, but when the time came, daddy wanted no part of it. So we didn't go ahead with it. Then Lucky seemed to get better, his hair was growing back, and he became more active. That's why we couldn't understand it.

Oh, Joe here it is 9:10 AM and I haven't done any work as yet, so I'd better get going on the letters I have rapidly accumulating in my work box. Take care and be good. Let me know if you need anything, okay? I'll write more next time.

Love, Sis

The above letters were waiting for me when we stood down.

October 7, 1971

Dear Dad,

Hi, how are you? I'm fine. I can't remember the last time I wrote you, so I guess it's time for another letter.

Today is re-supply day, and it's usually a good day. Now I am just sitting around waiting for all the good stuff to come in.

We've been on this mission for seven days already, seven more to go, then we go on stand-down, for a few days. Hoping our luck will hold out and the VC would behave for a few more days. 2 October, Election Day here in Nam. I guess you know more about the outcome than I do. But on that morning right down below our position, the VC fired off rockets, headed for Da Nang. Well, with artillery we stopped them after they got off six rockets. They could have been on timed fuses because the first one went off right at 6 AM and the others followed at intervals. We had an ambush set up for them the next night and got one NVA; he was still alive, but in bad shape. I didn't go out on the ambush; I stayed back and used my grenade launcher when the fireworks started. I feel safe carrying the M-203 around, it's definitely no toy.

We've been getting rain out here quite often, it rains two or three times a day. There is a tropical storm headed this way and hopefully we will be ready for it. How is the weather there? I bet all the trees are turning now and the fall season is in full swing. It's going to be strange not having any snow during the winter months over here. I guess I won't notice it for everything seems so unreal here.

I haven't received any packages yet. It could be that they're in the rear and I won't know until I go in. They don't bring packages out in the field; Sis wrote and told me you sent two packages rather than everything in one. That was a good idea, the mail system being what it is.

I didn't mention this before but I could use a knife out here, it would be a helpful item because I'm always looking for something sharp. The kind I could use is a straight hunting knife with a strong blade and case. I'm sure you know what kind I mean, a pocket knife is useless, as it wouldn't have the durability a hunting knife has. Also get a whetstone for sharpening. You could get it at the same place you buy the knife. Any hardware store should have just what I need. The cost, I don't know? Whatever it costs I'll be glad to pay you back. Okay? I hope you'll be able to send the knife to me soon. It will help me out a lot.

I've been getting a lot of mail lately. Aunt Pauline writes often, even the twins. I imagine Christine's wedding will be nice, I wish I could go. I also got a letter from mom's Aunt Ruth Young. I was sure surprised to hear from her. She sent me some religious materials that I didn't think too much of. Remember, I wrote and told you about the guy who told me about "being saved", and before you could go to heaven, you have to be "born again". Well, she sent me the same stuff. I'll send it to you and let you read it. Then you can dispose of it. It's not bad literature, but I can't believe it could be the true word of God.

I wrote Tom a letter about a week and a half ago. I got thinking how I have never written him since I've been in the Army. I think a lot of him and miss him. He is at a strange age now, and for him to know he is needed and loved by all of us is important.

Well Dad, I guess I'll end here. I hope your legs are all right these days. Take good care of yourself and my thoughts and prayers are with you all, always. Write me soon. Love, Joey

October 9, 1971

Dear Dad,

Hi, how are you? I got your letter dated 30 September. I was very glad to hear from you. I wrote you a few days ago and mentioned a hunting knife. I hope you were able to find one. I sure can use one out here in the bush.

I appreciate your sending me stuff, but as yet, I have not received anything. Perhaps I'll have packages waiting for me when I return to the rear. I go back on the 14th, so I should know how long it takes to receive it. I'll let you know then.

You mentioned that you received my check and you were going to put the money in an account for me. Dad, I would consider it a favor if you would use the money I send for the payments. It's no burden on me whatsoever, but the way Nixon is fouling up the U. S. Economy, I wouldn't want to burden you. So please take these checks and use them for the car and anything over $75 a month, you should keep. Remember that two dollars a day when I was going to school? That really ran into some money! I'll never be able to pay back the money you spent on me, I'll always remember it, and what a generous person you are.

I checked up on the picture I had taken, the first of this month, and they had just sent it off. You should get it soon.

I've been getting mail regularly from Aunt Pauline and the girls. I am well-informed about the wedding, and their excitement seems to be growing by each letter. I'm glad you're all going. It's unfortunate you couldn't stay until Thanksgiving.

Well, nothing new is happening around here. Are they still telling the American public that all the troops are standing down, and there is no more ground troops left in Nam? I sit out here and read this in the Army Times and the Stars & Stripes and think how deceiving the news media really is. They are telling me I'll be out of Nam the first of the year and I know I'll be out on some mission, deep in the bush, the first of the year. Somebody ought to wake the American people up. I don't think I'm going to read any newspapers when I come home, maybe the funnies that's about it, oh well.

Dad, take care of yourself, I'll write you again soon. Your thoughtfulness means much to me. Say hello to everyone.

Love, Joey

I mentioned my Aunt Pauline and the girls, let me explain; my Aunt Pauline was a prolific letter writer as long as I could remember. Back in the 50s and 60s letter writing was an art and my Aunt was Picasso. The girls I mentioned were my cousins Judy and Christine, Aunt Pauline's youngest (twin) daughters. Their older sister Leslie also wrote. I really appreciated their letters. I wasn't forgotten after all.

October 12, 1971

Hi Joey,

We got a letter today it wasn't too good to hear that you are heading out to the bush, watch out for booby-traps and be sure not to touch anything no matter how good it looks.

All is all right here. Suzanne has a bad cold and has been out of work for a couple of days. She's coming around now, maybe going back to work tomorrow. If not she might as well make a week of it.

Your car is in good shape, I had it going tonight and it seems to be as good as you left it, if it sits too long in one spot the brakes kind of hold, but it will break loose.

Panzie said he will write, we saw him last week and gave him your address. He said his water bill has gone way down since you stopped washing your car, but outside of that he's all right.

I got all the checks and I will deposit them in your savings account. Don't worry about the car we'll take care of it and the payments. Try to enjoy yourself while you are there. What I mean is don't run yourself short of money.

Love Dad

PS. I sent the letter and all pertinent info to Ham Fish and said that if necessary, a copy would be sent to the President.

Keep your chin up and don't worry, everything here is okay. I'll have Tom write. Will write again soon.

This was great news, the letter sent to (Ham Fish), Rep. Hamilton Fish Jr., Congressman from our Congressional District back home. It was a request for the U.S. Congress to approve and facilitate a Congressional Inquiry to the state of my health while in Vietnam. This had been ongoing before I entered the Army. My civilian doctor had written a letter addressed to the Selective Service Department stating his objection to my being drafted into the service. I presented this letter to the Selective Service upon reporting for induction;

they read it, and within an hour I was on my way to Fort Dix, New Jersey, my request for dismissal was denied.

I was ten years old, when diagnosed with a rare blood disorder requiring many hospital admissions, tests and doctor visits. I was operated on by Dr. Luby, who successfully removed my perfectly healthy spleen. The spleen is a filter that removes and destroys abnormal red blood cells. I was born with mis-shaped (abnormal) red blood cells and my spleen was destroying them at a rapid rate. This condition caused me to become weaker and weaker. If I scraped my knee, it took months for it to scab over and much longer for it to heal. I struggled with this disease from the age of 2 when I started to show symptoms. I was sickly, jaundice and in poor health; unfortunately, it took several years to diagnose my condition. My mother was relentless in her pursuit to find a cure for my condition. Finally, Dr. Luby from the Flower and Fifth Avenue Hospital, in New York City, made the diagnosis. Once the spleen was removed, my mother saw life come back to me. She said it was a miracle. I continued to improve, I was growing, my jaundice complexion improved, and I started living a normal life. I had some minor side effects but nothing like before.

I would visit Dr. Luby several times during the first few years. He would check my red blood cell count and other related blood issues.

When I got my draft notice, I immediately made an appointment to see Dr. Luby. After a lengthy discussion about my condition, he told me I was prone to pneumonia as a result of not having a spleen. I was told excessive bleeding could occur if I got seriously injured. I could become weakened or highly stressed, among other things. The letter he wrote, and I submitted to the Selective Service, stated all of these facts, along with his recommendation of non-combat duty. The letter disappeared and his recommendations disregarded. Nixon needed warm bodies in Nam, and that was that!

So, my Dad had requested the Congressional Inquiry.

Before I go any further, right around this time I received a letter from my sister including a copy of the letter my father sent to Congressman Fish, requesting the Congressional Inquiry.

September 23, 1971

Dear Joey,

Hi kid, how's it going? You know last night I had a dream that you came home for the weekend and it seemed so real. I feel as though I had a nice visit with you. I guess seeing you in a dream is better than not at all, huh? Well, we got two letters from you last night and I was sorry to hear you are not feeling well. As soon as Dad read that part where you asked his opinion on writing Ham Fish, he sat right down and put his thoughts down on paper. I typed it up for him today at work and I'll enclose a copy to let you know what Dad said. At this point I am pretty skeptical about getting any results, but at least you know we will be trying to help and make it easier for you. Maybe this time...

We sent you a package the other day and I think I got the main things you asked for and a few extras that might be useful. I don't know how long it will be before you receive it with the mail system being what it is. We divided the food stuff up and send two packages, so expect to receive another one about the time your first one arrives, okay?

Joe, I know you have been sending a lot of money home, but I'm wondering whether you're keeping enough for yourself. A lot of guys who've been to Vietnam invest in all kinds of stereo equipment, recording equipment, cameras, etc. Have you seen anything along these lines you'd be interested in? If so, it will give you something specific to save up for and give you hours of pleasure once you get it. Also, if you get a tape recorder, you can tape your voice and send the tapes home. I'd love to get something like that. It's something to think about, anyway.

Well, it's getting close to closing time, and I'll finish up the note and write more tomorrow or the next day. I know how important it is that you hear from home even if it's just to say hello, so I'll try to keep the letters coming frequently, okay doll. Take very good care of yourself and eat as much as you can hold at your meals. Maybe you'll feel better if you do. Missing you.... Love Sis

I was glad to get this letter, and thanks to my sister's secretarial training, she copied me on the following letter. I felt she missed me and her dream was interesting. I had visited home often while in basic training, but once I went to Fort Polk, Louisiana, coming home on a weekend pass was not possible. The recent letters they received from me probably sparked the dream. Anyway, it was good to know I wasn't forgotten, being isolated from your loved ones can be very lonely.

September 23, 1971

Dear Mr. Fish:

My name is Joseph J. Freeborn, a disabled veteran of World War II, two years a POW of Hitler.

My son, Joseph, at the age of 10 was operated on for the complete removal of the spleen, which had been causing severe anemia since he was age two. Upon completion of this operation, he was informed that he would never have the stamina of a normal adult male.

Last March he was called by the draft, at which time he submitted a statement of his medical history to the Draft Board. Joe was willing to serve his country; all he asked was that he be given responsibilities which would not be detrimental to his health, in view of his past medical history. We obtained an opinion from the operating surgeon and were informed that should Joe receive a major wound two possibilities were presented; uncontrollable bleeding and abnormal susceptibility to infectious disease. With this testimony evident, the Army saw fit to commit this boy into the worst possible conditions. According to the last letter we received from Vietnam, Joe is now experiencing the same conditions as Dr. Luby warned against, weakness, lack of physical stamina.

My son is not trying to evade duty to his country and only asks in all fairness and justice that his physical condition be taken into consideration. How many perfectly healthy men are now stationed in Europe and other non-combat zones of the world? Joe was not a "long hair" and he doesn't have the affluence of a Cassius Clay, but God, he has a love for his family and country and is a good American, brought up in the tradition of justice and is willing with all his strength to preserve the nation from its enemies. Is the Army trying to shake his belief in American justice?

I expect an early reply.

Sincerely,

Joseph J. Freeborn

It is important to know that my family struggled under the weight of my illness. For about 2 years it was doctor's visits, hospital stays and misdiagnoses. When I was in Flower and Fifth Avenue Hospital, my mother stayed in New York City, and my Dad had to take care of everything at home.

My Dad's letter to Congressman Fish was a passionate plea to save my life. My mother had so diligently stood by me with my illness; he in turn continued to fight for my survival. That is how I read this letter. I was the son he had the most hope in. I was his fair-haired boy, his name sake. I knew that's how he felt.

October 12, 1971

Dear Dad,

Hi, how are you? I received your letter today, and it was good hearing from you. Yes, I am feeling much better lately. Right now however, I'm back in the rear, with some sores on my arm. I thought I would come in and get them cleaned up. The Doc gave me some penicillin to take, and they are going away. It's a common ailment in the field, we call it "jungle rot" but it's not really. The Army terms it "cellulitis" I had it on my elbow, it made the movement of my arm difficult. It's better now, so no sweat.

I also received a letter from Sister Mary Margaret yesterday. I wrote her back already. I like getting mail from her; she is very sincere. Do you write her often? I cannot lose, with your prayers and Sister's, and Angie's, I feel safe. I remember all of you in my daily prayers.

I haven't gotten any packages as yet. They have a lot of packages stored away somewhere and are waiting for the Company to come in on the 14th. I'll probably get it then.

Well Dad, I'll end here. I wrote Tom a letter a few weeks ago and await his reply. How is he doing? Take care of yourself and give my best to all.

Love, Joey

I was shamming as we called it. I hopped onto a re-supply chopper a few days ago to get my arm looked at, "jungle rot," as Doc called it. "Could get infected," he said, and called for evac. The mission was almost over, the guys would come in soon; we never knew exactly when.

After a few days I was back with my squad. I was struggling out in the bush, and this incident was a warning sign, more would follow.

During this time, I was feeling the ill effects of being a grunt, the environment was hostile, and the accumulating effects of these conditions were taking hold.

Earlier in this mission we had an unfortunate incident, as the Army refers to it, but really it was a tragic loss of life. Friendly fire killed this new guy. His name was Robert Goodman Jr. He was very new in-country, and I suspect he was struggling with the reality of Vietnam. My brief observation of him was he seemed isolated, and I wanted to reach out to him as others had done to me; unfortunately, that never happened. The last thing I remember was his boots hanging out of the open side door of the chopper. I recall thinking, he was going home.

Over the years I thought about him, and I record the following information, as written by the U.S. Army.

Robert O. Goodman, Jr. residing at and was educated in Tamcliff, West Virginia, during his youth and died in service to his country in the United States Army on October 3, 1971, as a result of a gunshot to the head, fired by another soldier near the mountain of Nui Son Ga, 20 miles northwest of Hoi An City, in Quang Nam Province, Republic of Vietnam; he was buried at the Hollywood Cemetery in Gilbert, West Virginia.

Chapter 10

October 18, 1971

Dear Dad,

I received your letter, and it was good hearing from you. I wrote you a few days ago. I have good news to tell you, I'm coming home. I really can't wait until I leave this place. Although I must return, it will still be great getting home again. I'll feel so safe and I'll be glad to see you all again.

I'll be getting free transportation from Vietnam to Hawaii. I must pay the rest of the way. It shouldn't be too expensive; I'm figuring about $300 round trip.

I'm glad my car is all right. Have you put it away yet? I guess the weather isn't that bad, but before you know it, you might have an inch of snow on the ground. I hope you'll have the car under cover before that. You also mentioned receiving the treasury checks. I wrote you about them a few letters ago; I hope you understand what I'm trying to say. The car is my responsibility, not yours. I don't want to burden you with my obligations, okay?

I'll be putting the items you sent me to good use in a few days. The monsoon season is in full swing. It's raining a lot, but not constantly yet. It's raining right now but will stop soon. We go back out after our six-day stand down in two more days, the 20th. The soup will really taste good out there. The hot chocolate is ideal. The Army has something like it, but you don't get enough of it. The coffee that comes with the c-rats is disgusting. If you put a lot of sugar in it, and the water is really hot, it's drinkable. Otherwise it makes me sick. I appreciate everything you sent, thanks again.

Well Dad, I've got to end here. I hope this letter finds you and everyone well. I hope Sis is feeling better by now. Tell her to take care of herself. I will write to her soon. Write again, when you can.

Love, Joey

October 19, 1971

Dear Sis,

Well, here I am again, told you I'd write again soon. Not really however, I had just put the earlier letter in the mail and I got a package. The one with the tapes. This is a thank you note. I really like both tapes, and with my new tape player, will sound real good. I sold my small one for

$25 and bought a second-hand one for $20. It's a better player with AM/FM radio. Good deal don't you think? I just so happen to know what "gratis" means. I'm not as stupid as you think! Thanks a lot.

Well, tomorrow it's back to work, I'm dreading the hassle, but once I'm out there, it's no sweat. I'm hoping the rain keeps up however, and I don't want it to come down, all over me. I hate being wet! Well Sis, I better end here, write me when you can, okay?

Love, Joey

PS. Say hi to all for me.

I received the following letters the next day, re-supply day.

October 19, 1971

Hi Joey,

I got your letter dated October 9, two days ago, so the mail delivery isn't too bad. Everything here is okay, Panzie (owner of Gulf service station) was asking for you and he promised to write. Joe Pendolino (neighbor) was just over and gave us haircuts. Tom didn't have much taken off and I couldn't spare much, so he made short work of it, he wasn't here too long.

Got another bond yesterday, I think it's the fourth one, they're always good and the longer you keep them, the better they are.

As far as the money you sent, don't worry, I'll put as much as I can into the account you have with the bank. I don't need the money and I'll save it, it'll come in handy when you get home. Also, if you want any part of the farm to build on, it's yours, pick out the best spot and take as much as you want. Building is going on like crazy in Marlborough, the houses are going up like mushrooms, you won't know the place.

I will send the knife you wanted Thursday, I don't know what you're hunting but if you want it, I'll send a good one.

I'll be looking forward to getting the picture; you say it should arrive soon. I'm also glad Pauline and the girls have been writing; I knew she would. We are all looking forward to the wedding. I don't care much for these productions, but it seems to be the thing today, so we'll have a good time.

Pres. Nixon is trying to pull the troops from what we hear, and the South Vietnam troops are filling in the gap and taking most of the guff, this is the way it should be, and I hope it's true.

144

The weather here has been good these past couple of weeks, a little cool and foggy in the morning, but sunny most of the day.

I got the cover for the car. I'll get Tom to wash it and then cover it with this felt I have and then put the plastic cover over it. It should be in good shape when you get home. I'll try to keep it running as long as I can before the snow.

I miss you Joey take care of yourself and watch those booby-traps.

Love, Dad

That last sentence caused me to pause, it was the first time my Dad said <u>he</u> missed me.

October 22, 1971

Hi Joey,

Well, we got the great news tonight, and it sure was a surprise hearing you can get out of there for a while. This is the best word we've heard from that place.

We'll surely be down to get you when you land in N.Y. Just give me the date, and we'll be there.

I sent the knife and some other snacks in a package today and I hope it reaches you soon.

It was nice of Ruth Young (Mom's aunt in Arkansas) to write you and I'm sure the literature she sent you is harmless and might be of some comfort to you. She is a good woman and if the world had more people like her, it wouldn't be in this shape. You never met her, but we spent quite some time with her.

Everything is okay here, this is Friday night and we're all a little tired after a big week, so I'll get this off to you to let you know how happy the news was, take care.

Love, Dad

October 30, 1971

Dear Dad,

I received two letters from you recently one dated the 19th and the other dated 22nd. It was sure good hearing from you.

It sounds like all is going well at home, and I can't complain over here. We're getting a lot of rain, but yesterday the sun came out. We are back out in the bush, and I'm getting to where I consider the bush home. I've spent about 95% of the three months I've been here out in the sticks.

I'm just about out of the soup you sent. It sure was great, I enjoyed it very much. Perhaps you could send more. Okay? I'll also need batteries for a Kodak Instamatic 44. The batteries look like little disks, about the size of a quarter. They are not available over here, and without them I'm limited to daytime pictures only. I hope to fill a whole album while I'm here.

I'm glad the news of my coming home made you all happy. I'm overjoyed with the idea. I'm scheduled to leave January 1, but they might delay me. If everything goes as planned, you'll get a phone call from me probably from California. It should be early afternoon on January 1. It will sure be good to be home again.

I'm glad you found a knife without too much trouble, I'll be glad to get it.

It sounds like you've got my car pretty well squared away. Thanks for taking care of it. I sent $80 home this month. I wanted to buy Angie a birthday present also, but they are still taking out $100 for some kind of class E allotment (not mine). I will get it straightened out when I go back in on 7 November. They had better make good on the $200 bucks.

Well, Dad I'd better end here. I have more letters to write, one to Sister Mary Margaret, she writes quite a bit. Oh, she sent me this envelope for a contribution to the Mission of Our Lady of Mercy. I'll send the envelope with this letter, please enclose five dollars, make sure you use my money, okay? Thanks.

Take care of yourself and don't worry about me. I'm doing all right.

Write soon.

Love, Joey

I wrote the following letter, this was the second unanswered letter to my kid brother, Tom.

October 30, 1971

Dear Tom,

How are you? I've been waiting and waiting for a letter from you, but I don't seem to be getting one. I decided to write you again, hoping you'll get the hint. I sure would like hearing from you. You have never written me a letter you know.

Well everything on this side of the world is alright. There isn't much fighting going on over here, at the present. We're mostly trying to keep safe, but we do go out looking for "dinks" once in a while. They are pretty sneaky and hard to find. The only way to know they have been around is by the booby traps they leave for us. Yesterday we found a claymore mine sitting on the trail, we blew it in place, for fear it might have a secondary charge attached to it. The claymore itself is ours, but the dinks have "policed" some of them up, those we left lying around. They would put 500 pound B-52 bombs under them with a pressure release firing device to detonate the bomb. I've never seen the outcome, but I image it would be a "blast". I don't play around with booby traps at all, when one is found I find a large rock or tree, and sit there until it's blown up. I'm no fool!

How is school coming? Do you like the new high school? It's quite a place. I'll be looking forward to hearing all about it. I bet if you wanted to, you could write me a small book about your first year in high school.

I'll probably be home for your birthday, or close to it. I'm hoping I'll be able to leave Nam 1 January, but I might be delayed. They have a lot of nice tape recorders and radios over here. There are a lot of cassette tape players; do you still like to fool around with recording stuff? If so, let me know and I'll bring you a nice tape player or something for your birthday. You have to let me know though.

Well Tom, I'll end here. I do want to hear from you, so write me, okay? Take care and say hello to everyone for me.

Joey

I promised Tom my car if he returned to school and graduated; that never happened. He wrote me once, and I never wrote him again. I felt a sense of loss not hearing much from Tom and nothing from my brother Jeff, not one word from him all the time I was in Nam.

I had to get my "shit" together and make my flight arrangements soon. It was early November, and the paperwork needed to leave Vietnam seemed overwhelming. I was out in the bush 22-24 days a month and everything I needed to do was on Freedom Hill near our base camp. I had to get these things done when I got back to the rear. I couldn't wait to see everyone again; I thought it might be the last time.

Being in Vietnam was a life and death situation, it had hardened me. I resigned myself to the fact that death or serious injury was eminent. I had seen too much to believe I would skate through this mess. Vietnam was winding down and the anti-war sentiment was heating up. The protesters back home smelled blood in the water, and the White House was considering their re-election chances. This war was being fought from the Oval Office, not by the generals in the field. As a grunt in a combat zone, you could not have your hands tied behind your back. That's how we felt sometimes, making this phase of the Vietnam War very dangerous for the 70,000 remaining troops.

The Jane Fonda's were winning, and we were trying to survive. We could not refuse to fight this war; we had taken an oath to serve our country, an oath our military took seriously. If we had protested our involvement and refused to go out to the bush, we would do hard time in Ft. Leavenworth Military Prison. We had raised our hand and swore to protect and defend the United States of America against foreign and domestic threats. Vietnam was a foreign threat to our democracy.

Early the next morning, Festus told me I was walking slack, he would be walking point. I rarely walked point or slack, being the squad grenadier. I swapped my M-203 with Speed's M-16. The patrol formation would change depending on the mission. Today it was my turn in the second most dangerous spot, slack!

Before leaving our NDP, I noticed Festus was unusually quiet; he sat down, leaned up against his ruck, and honed his machete. I observed the intensity of his actions as he skillfully sharpened the machete he'd use to hack through the thick jungle growth. The terrain was comprised of dense thicket, with heavy bamboo and reed grass. He knew he would need a super sharp machete today. After a while, he got up, strapped on his ruck and growled, "Let's move out."

It was difficult to see through the heavy vegetation. I was straining to see anything ahead. Festus was chopping and hacking our way through, I was his eyes and ears. I had to react immediately if I heard or saw anything ahead of him. The guys behind me were looking right and left for any sign of VC. Ambushes were always on our mind when patrolling.

Oh shit, "Festus, what the hell?" I whispered loudly.

My left hand index finger was squirting blood. Festus had slipped, and his machete caught my finger just right. It cut the flesh to the bone.

"Get Doc up here," Festus ordered.

The wound was significant, cut to the bone, and the bleeding was nonstop. Doc wrapped it using a whole roll of gauze, taped it up, and I mumbled something like, "don't mean nothing", let's go.

Time was wasting, we had ground to cover. We continued, Festus at point and me at slack, at least for a few minutes.

I happened to look down at my bandage and saw blood dripping from the tip of my left pinky finger; the bleeding had not stopped. The gauze was red, saturated with blood.

"Hey Festus, let's hold up," I said.

Doc Shaw came back up to the front of the column, removing the dressing, he declared, "I can't stop the bleeding."

I immediately recalled that excessive bleeding might occur because of my blood disorder. I became more concerned; the wound was serious and I did not want to bleed out. Doc applied an upper arm tourniquet, it helped a little.

"What should we do Doc?" Festus inquired.

"Get Danny (our radio man) up here," Doc Shaw said. "We have to call LT."

Doc Shaw reported the situation to LT. Clark (Gary Clark), our acting CO. Clark asked me how I was feeling. I told him I was "okay, but this damn finger is fucked up."

After a slight pause he came back on and ordered Festus to have the squad cut an LZ, "Freeborn has to be med-evac'd out of the bush."

I felt a little silly watching my squad cut through the shit so a chopper could set down. They had called the chopper and it would be here soon. Doc kept applying pressure at certain points along my arm and the bleeding slowed down, almost to a drip. But as soon as he released pressure, it would bleed again with no sign of stopping. Once he found the spot he was looking for, he told me to keep pressure there until I got back to the rear. "I'll notify them, they'll know what to do," Doc reassured me.

I heard the chopper blades cutting through the dense heavy air. I could not believe the chopper was coming for me. I was lucky I thought, but felt awkward having everyone make such a fuss. They helped me onto the chopper, and threw my rucksack in after me. Festus handed me my M-203 and smiled, "good luck man."

A medic on board the chopper was expecting the worst. He attended to my wound as best he could, and seemed relieved it was only cut. A few minutes later we were back in the rear.

The new rear area had a fully equipped medical facility, not a hospital, but rather a large emergency clinic, like a MASH unit. They had kept it intact after the Marines left, and now served the Army units in the immediate area. My treatment consisted of a butterfly bandage and no stitches. My hand was completely wrapped up, and I was assigned limited duty. The medic told me to report to my First Sergeant with the orders for restricted duty. I was out of the bush for 3 days and would have to report back to the clinic in 2 days before returning to regular duty.

I gave the folder to our new Company Clerk, Sweeney. He took the folder, looked up at me and asked, "how's the finger?"

"Fine, I think I'll survive," I replied.

He continued, "I'll get this to Top (First Sergeant). Get your gear together," pointing to the floor. Someone had brought all my stuff to his office. I gathered everything up as he continued, "go up to Building 3, you'll see some other guys up there."

I turned in my weapon and ammo, checked in with supply for clean clothes, towels, toiletries, etc., and made my way up the hill to Building 3.

After settling in, I showered trying to keep my hand dry and changed into clean clothes. Lying on my bunk, I felt uneasy. I replayed the recent events in my head. The quietness of the near empty barracks seemed strange as did my surroundings. I had just been taken out of the bush, separated from my squad, my family and now alone. In Nam, you became dependent on familiar things, like the bush, your squad and the firepower you carried. For me, this was my security, this was my safe place. Not here, where anything could happen, and you had no defense, no weapon, not even a bayonet, that had to be turned in too.

I wondered what the guys were doing, probably looking for an NDP. At least I won't have that to deal with tonight. I thought of Doc Shaw, how attentive and concerned he was, and the look on Festus' face when he saw the blood streaming from my finger. I also envisioned my team members cutting that LZ. They cared about me I thought. I would never forget that!

The next days were uneventful. I went back to the clinic and had the wound re-dressed. I needed a few more days before returning to the bush. It was a deep cut, and could open up again if not healed properly. I went back to the Company area with the results of my exam and found out the Company was coming back in the next day. They would be in for a short stand-down and then we were going to China Beach. Wow, I thought, China Beach what the hell was that? It sounded good; I knew the guys needed a break from the shit.

Chapter 11

They scrapped the China Beach mission; we were to head out to a remote region called Monkey Mountain, about 25 clicks (kilometers) northwest of Da Nang.

Reportedly there was a large buildup of NVA in that region, and guess what, it was our turn to mix it up with them. Our sister company, Co. C, had encountered an insurgent force of NVA, and had been pinned down for 72 hours, with multiple causalities reported. All this "intel" was by word of mouth, rumors or gossip, take your pick.

We came into a hot LZ; it was about 1400 hours, and the sun was slowly settling down on the tree-lined horizon. I thought this mission was starting late, but what did I know? As the choppers came in, one at a time, the 3rd chopper was drawing enemy fire; the guys on the ground were returning fire. I was on the 4th chopper, as we approached the LZ, they informed us we had to jump out; the chopper was not setting down. As my feet hit the soft mushy turf, I sank up to my knees in mud. I looked up, only to see the 5th chopper coming in right over me, and he was setting the chopper down closer to the

158

ground. I struggled to get out of the way of the descending chopper skids, but I couldn't. I pulled on the emergency release straps and broke free from my rucksack and rolled my body away from the chopper. It missed me by inches, and I could still hear M-16 fire coming from the wood line. I continued to free myself from the mud, grabbed my rucksack and made my way to the perimeter, joining the other guys.

The small arms fire stopped, and as usual, the VC were gone. We collected ourselves, grouped off into squads, and made our way to our NDP. It was almost dark and I had all to do to get my NDP set up, constructing the usual makeshift tent/hammock sleeping position. I ate something convenient and tried to get some rest, guard duty would start soon. I lucked out and got early duty; I was hoping to get some sleep; I was beat.

We were at full strength now, our Company and our squads were properly manned. We had a few new guys join us during our last stand down, and I felt more at ease out here. We had a new CO (Company Commander) and some of the older guys stayed in the rear or were reassigned to the CP (Command Post). I was now one of the senior guys in my squad, and I noticed the newbies were asking me questions, the same questions I had asked just a few months earlier. That's how it was, a war of attrition. We were the replacements which allowed the older guys to go home. I understood that concept, and couldn't wait for my replacement to arrive in country.

LT. Clark was our Platoon Leader; he would decide which squads would patrol where. We moved in a specific pattern and were in constant contact via our radio operator Dan Gerleve. He would shadow LT. Clark while on patrol. LT. would rotate within the three squads. Dan would now be assigned to CP.

We moved around the AO without too much trouble. No NVA activity, just signs of past VC activity. They usually left souvenirs for us to find, such as booby traps, bungee pits, bamboo spiked catapult, etc. There would be the occasional "bouncing Betty" land mine. These devices were pressure sensitive once stepped on and released; the mine would bounce up, knee high, and ruin the rest of your day. I only saw one actual example of a bouncing Betty, it was horrific; Dave Leone survived, but probably never walked again, his tour of duty ended that day.

The rest of that day we patrolled the rivers and streams, climbed Monkey Mountain, and made our way back down through stream beds and dried up tributaries. It was dry and water was getting harder to find. That was all about to change as rain was predicted with stronger southwesterly winds. Typhoon Hester was coming our way. I had never experienced a typhoon or a hurricane. I didn't know what to expect, but soon we would be right in the middle of it. Our mission was scheduled for about 10 days, and we had just gotten out there. I had hoped the storm would hold off until we got back in, but that was wishful thinking!

After a few days they decided the whole Company would assemble near the top of Monkey Mountain. It was well camouflaged and densely wooded. The foliage would hide us and the elevation would keep us from getting flooded out. The rain was relentless, and the winds were getting steadier and stronger. The sky above us was brownish gray, ominous would best describe it.

We all got busy hunkering down. We constructed a couple of large shelters using our ponchos tied together and secured to sturdy trees. This was not the norm as we never clustered together (cluster fuck) under normal conditions; but this was an emergency. About 4-6 guys would occupy each shelter, getting as comfortable inside as possible. There wasn't a lot of room, but we would have to make do.

The storm was worsening, and the winds were getting stronger. The rain was now coming down sideways, pulling and tugging at our makeshift shelters. One shelter finally let loose from its tether, and we watched 4 guys trying to gather it up. They got it back together and tied it off securely this time.

Typhoon Hester lasted for about 24 hours before the winds subsided. The rain kept coming, keeping us supplied with drinking water. We would put our canteen cups outside and they would fill quickly. Our food was running low, and some guys were almost out. They postponed re-supply hoping conditions would improve. We waited and waited, with no word from base camp. Radio communication was sketchy, and we were nowhere near the CP squad. The storm was much more severe near the coast, and our rear area was only a few clicks from the South China Sea.

Another full day and night passed, and we were still hunkered down. The storm was losing its punch and the rain would stop from time to time. Our food supplies had dwindled and I was completely out, living on some soda crackers and rain water. I was hungry for the first time in my life. Food was becoming a pre-occupation for me, that's all I thought about.

Festus stopped by our tent and said re-supply would be tomorrow morning, conditions had improved at base camp, and choppers were no longer grounded. We waited all morning, but the chopper never came. It was mid-afternoon; I was getting hungrier with each passing hour. I tried not thinking about food, but real hunger is a funny thing; food and eating becomes an obsession and difficult to ignore.

Bird-in-bound someone yelled, then the order to pop smoke. The long awaited re-supply was finally happening, the LZ was very rugged, and the terrain was un-level. The chopper was struggling to set down as there were lots of large trees and rocks where it was attempting to land. As the chopper set down, the tail rotor got caught on a tree branch and the chopper rotated out of control. The tail rotor keeps the aircraft steady, and once that tail rotor stops, the chopper begins to spin around uncontrollably. The pilot did his best, but the chopper was too far gone; it flipped over and dove into the ground. It was a nightmare.

The chopper was upside down with its nose buried in the underbrush. The tail rotor was visibly damaged and everything inside the chopper was all over the place. We went to the smoldering wreckage, trying to help the passengers. The Company Clerk and Top were in there as were the pilots. We could safely remove everyone, except for one pilot who was severely injured and later died. Doc Shaw and the other medics treated the injured passengers. The rest of us cleared a better LZ a few meters from the original one. The injured men had to get airlifted out and needed medical attention. That was the first real DUSTOFF mission I had seen.

DUSTOFF–Dedicated Unhesitating Service To Our Fighting Force

Dustoff in Vietnam was a crew of four dedicated (most would say certifiably insane) men that flew unarmed helicopters to the front line and beyond to rescue wounded soldiers.

Their mission was to get wounded soldiers out of harm's way, save their life by providing basic medical treatment while en-route to the nearest and best hospital.

Many of these unarmed, clearly marked Arial Ambulances got shot down, and many of their crews perished in pursuit of their mission.

We secured the crash site, armed and ready to protect the asset, the chopper. As with any military crash, the sites had to be investigated and reported on in great detail. Our charge was to secure the site and await further orders from high command. An investigation team would arrive, along with the recovery chopper. It wasn't too long, about an hour, when we saw the Chinook double propped helicopter come in view. This helicopter was huge, and would remove the crashed chopper and bring it back to the rear for further investigation. Because a fatality had occurred and there were multiple injuries, this investigation would be thorough.

A small unit of about 6 men repelled from the hovering Chinook, and at once set up a perimeter around the crashed chopper. They were heavily armed and said nothing to us. Two of the men went to work rigging up heavy steel cables that were dropped from the Chinook, attaching the cables at the proper lift point on the wrecked fuselage. Within minutes the chopper was lifted and suspended. The men on the ground were winched up into the Chinook. The entire operation only took 15-20 minutes, these men were well trained, and apparently they had done this before. A few minutes later the flying spectacle was gone; we all watched in shock and disbelief.

Slowly, we moved around the crash site, picking up everything. The VC would be in here right after we leave, so we couldn't overlook anything. There wasn't anything worth salvaging, all the food was destroyed, and the dry clothes were soaked with water and jet fuel. Our hot meal was totally destroyed. I could not believe nothing had survived, but nothing did. I was hungry and would have eaten anything, but there was nothing left. It was all destroyed.

Early the next morning, Festus informed us of a re-supply scheduled for later today. We would have to stay here a little longer having successfully carved out a suitable LZ. He also asked any of us who had any c-rats or LRPPs to share them with the guys who were out. You see, they trained us to be self-sufficient, for a variety of reasons, but survival was always reason number 1. Some guys were quick to share what little they had, while the old timers hesitated, survival, remember?

We continued this convoluted mission once re-supply was over. Yes, we got our re-supply and had plenty to eat. No mail, as they held it back in the rear. We needed food and supplies, not mail. We moved out of our familiar area, and the rest of the mission was uneventful. Many of us recounted the things that had happened, "shit, that was some fuckin' storm," seemed to be the general consensus.

I had no access to the news of that day, and I had no idea of the severity of this typhoon. I didn't even know it had a name, Hester. They told us we had to hunker down where we were. When I wrote this book, I researched various sources and came up with the following summary of events and damage because of this typhoon:

The storm killed 36 people which included 3 Americans.

The storm was concentrated in five northern most provinces in South Vietnam.

It left many thousands of people homeless and the storm damaged several combat bases.

The winds exceeded 130 mph and made landfall in Chu Lai, located 350 miles northeast of Saigon.

90% of crops were destroyed in some areas of the provinces affected.

The Americal Division Headquarters in Chu Lai was severely damaged affecting 75% of the base.

The American Air Base in Da Nang was also severely damaged as it sat right on the coastline of the South China Sea. Several roofs were blown off, and it damaged or destroyed some aircraft hangars. The

Airfield remained open throughout the storm running on emergency generators.

There was no combat related activity during the storm, even the VC hunkered down, probably underground. The U.S. continued B-52 bombings of Laos and Cambodia, disrupting supply lines from North Vietnam to South Vietnam.

I'm pretty sure that the accidental death of the chopper pilot was not listed here as one of the 3 Americans killed. But, he was killed in the line of duty, in combat.

When we got back to the rear, the mood was somber, and we all seemed to be only going through the motions. Anytime we had a casualty within our company, we all mourned that death, and recommitted ourselves to each other, silently. That was the unwritten and unspoken contract of the "grunt" in Nam. We were not individuals, but a team, that had to work together and accomplish the mission, whatever it was. There was no place for slackers, druggies, or mental or physical weakness out in the bush. When one was hurting, we all were hurting. When one of us were missing, it was never unnoticed.

Chapter 12

We returned to the base camp, the days ran together and sometimes I'd lose track of days in the shuffle. It didn't matter as time seemed meaningless in Nam. We were serving a 12 month sentence, don't mean nothin'.

We were all beat up and needed to re-group. We had just been through an unbelievable week; this war had taken on a different feel. The weather kicked our ass, not Charlie. We experienced the awesome forces of Mother Nature, much more powerful than we expected. We lost a chopper pilot in a freak crash. They designate him KIA (killed in action) and, after a long Army career, he went home.

November 4, 1971

Dear Dad,

Hi, I received the package today, thanks a lot. The knife is just what I wanted. The other items will be useful as well.

At the present time, I'm in the rear. I had an accident and my left index finger got cut by a machete. A guy in front of me was cutting point; the blade slipped and caught my finger. It bled a lot, and I thought I needed stitches, but I didn't after all. It's coming along well, however.

There isn't much happening over here, at least at present. We're just putting in time, it seems. I'm up for Spec 4 promotion and should get it sometime this month.

Well, that's about all I can think of at the present. Thank you again for the package. Take care of yourself and give my best to all at home. Okay? I understand through one of Angie's letter, Uncle Harry had a heart attack, how is he? I'll probably write him soon. Bye for now!

Love, Joey

The order came down to move out the day after next. I think it was November 6th. They rotated us into China Beach to provide security for the 95th Evac Hospital. Company C had just been there and was now going on stand down. We had to move out before they returned as there wasn't enough room in the rear for more than one company at a time.

Upon arriving at China Beach, the sickening smell of human feces and warm salt air made me nauseous at first. The compound was impressive, with lots of low white buildings which housed medical personnel. There were various medical units, with specialties in skin disorders, snake bites and other field related abnormalities.

The beach was dirty and people walked back and forth on it. With no roads visible, I assumed they used the beach as their main thoroughfare. After a while, I noticed civilians dropping their draws to take a leak or dump, right there on the sand. Like cats, they'd cover their deposits with sand and move on. The constant ocean breeze delivered the stench to us on the other side of the razor wire fence. Like everything else in Nam, we got used to it.

The whole Company was there. They assigned us to teams which would man elevated watch towers surrounding the compound. There were rows of razor wire and concertina wire with obstacles like mounds and holes dug in the perimeter. This was all to prevent sapper attacks which occurred from time to time. We would occupy these towers 24 hours a day, with 12-hour shifts per team. There was no bathroom breaks or mess hall visits while on duty. We'd revert to our grunt ways of doing things while on duty. Time moved slowly, and it was boring. Conversations grew less frequent and all we could do was watch the locals walk up and down the beach. Sometimes they were entertaining, and we'd have a laugh occasionally. The sergeant-at-arms would check up on us, we had to be alert and challenge him when he came around. If we didn't, he could write us up for an Article 15; not being alert while on guard duty was bad news.

Offenses Punishable Under Article 15

To start Article 15 action, a commander must have reason to believe a member of his/her command committed an offense under the UCMJ (Uniform Code of Military Justice). Article 15 gives a commanding officer power to punish individuals for minor offenses. The term "minor offense" has caused concern in the administration of NJP. Article 15, UCMJ, and Part V, para, 1e, MCM (1998 ed.), show that the term "minor offense" means misconduct normally not more serious than that handled at summary court-martial (where the maximum is thirty days confinement). These sources also indicate that the nature of the offense and the circumstances surrounding its commission are also factors which should be considered in determining whether an offense is minor in nature. The term "minor offense" ordinarily does not include misconduct which, if tried by general court-martial, could be punished by a dishonorable discharge or confinement for more than one year. The military service, however, have taken the position that the final determination whether an offense is "minor" is within the sound discretion of the commanding officer.

This procedure was uncommon in Nam, but did happened. The whole experience was so objective and screwed up, that after a while, even Article 15 didn't matter. We were trying to survive and to serve honorably. Sometimes these conflicting emotions became blurred, so they handed out Article 15s, I almost got one.

I came close to getting written up for Article 15 after a difficult 24 day mission. I was extra dirty, irritated and somewhat brain dead. I did not go to the armory, and check my weapon and ammo. Instead of waiting on a long line outside the armory, I went to the barracks, showered, changed clothes then turn my stuff in. This was a bad decision however, and violated UCMJ (Uniform Code of Military Justice), under Article 15. I covered up my M-16 and stashed my ammo under a blanket. Dropped my rucksack on top of the bed and proceeded to the empty shower room.

Upon returning, my Platoon Sergeant Mac (Robert McKissic) greeted me with, "What the hell are you doing?"

He had uncovered my M-16. I knew full well weapons were not allowed in our living area when in the rear. I got caught and had no excuse.

Sergeant Mac, an older black man was a good guy. He had helped me one time out in the bush when I became weak and dizzy from heat stroke. He happened to be humping near me when I stumbled and fell down; I had become dehydrated, and it was hot that day. Mac tended to me and stayed with me. Doc monitored my situation, and after a while I felt better, and we proceeded on.

Mac continued to chew my ass out and threatened to write me up for this serious infraction. After some time, he relented and gave me a stern warning.

"Next time you fuck up, you'll see the Old Man."

It upset me that I got caught; pissed off for not living up to my personal standards of conduct. I never had another incident and learned a valuable lesson on obeying orders.

The chow at China Beach was great. They served most meals buffet style, and food seemed always available, 24 hours a day. With so many shifts, set chow times were impossible, so the buffet worked well for them. For us, it was like Thanksgiving dinner every day and we took full advantage.

Chapter 13

I hitched a ride with the supply sergeant; he was heading over to Freedom Hill. The airbase was on the way and he was good enough to give me a lift. I didn't know the guy, but I asked him for a ride anyway.

We pulled into the secured gated area before entering the air base, an MP asked for paperwork. In Vietnam, no one traveled without authorization or orders. I had a letter and travel voucher, to board the next C-130 to Tan Son Nhut, Saigon. The MP looked the paperwork over carefully, then waved us through the security gate. The Jeep traveled a short distance and stopped at a makeshift terminal; I jumped out and thanked him for the ride.

I had to wait about an hour before the C-130 was fueled and ready to go. There were about 10-12 other guys heading down south, and they loaded the plane with lots of cargo. The take-off was noisy and the in-flight noise wasn't much better. After a while I got use to the strange noises the plane made, as hydraulic pumps turned on and off and fluid raced through the hydraulic lines. The plane was really a troop and cargo transport. I sat on web seating hanging from the fuselage ceiling; it wasn't very comfortable. The trip took about an hour and a half, arriving a little after 1:00 PM.

Before I left the Company area, they issued me a new pair of fatigues and new boots. I kept my old ones, as I wasn't going back to the bush with new boots. Besides, the ones I replaced were just broken in. Apparently I had to look presentable to the higher ups in Saigon. They had given me strict orders to keep out of local establishments, and not to trust any of the locals. They'll kill you if they have the chance. Oh yeah, I'm still in Nam.

I checked in with the clerk at the reception counter in Saigon; he told me to report to the MACV Compound. He gave directions and mentioned taking a cab, but walking seemed safer. It wasn't that far, and I needed to walk around and survey my new surroundings. I noticed many taxi cabs around the airport, but I wasn't going to trust them, recalling my orders to keep to myself.

As I walked along the sidewalk which ran alongside a busy 4 lane roadway, I was amazed at the amount of traffic and the number of U.S. cars running around. I saw an almost new Ford Mustang, and I took a picture of it; it really took me by surprise. There were also late 50s and 60s U.S. cars and they looked like they had been there for a while. Up to now I had only seen motor scooters, bicycles and rickshaws running around up in Da Nang.

The MACV Compound resembled a roadside motel back home. It had two floors of exposed doors off a balcony, and wooden staircases on either end to access the upper floor. The place seemed well occupied and had an Olympic size swimming pool with tables and chaise lounges. The REMPS (rear echelon military personnel) stationed there had it made I thought. I wouldn't have traded places with them; I was a grunt, no matter how much I hated admitting it. I had been in country long enough now, and there was no turning back. Even as I continued to get relieved from combat duty, I would miss the shit; that is humping the bush. It's counterintuitive and hard to explain, but I was caught between wanting out and needing to stay with my unit, my family in Nam.

I hung around the compound taking in the sights, taking pictures and just trying to enjoy myself, but I felt conflicted. My team was without a grenadier and they were out in a fairly dangerous AO. I had to stay behind due to this trip. I felt strange when they left without me. No one knew I was going for a Congressional Inquiry medical exam, at least no one that mattered.

Festus knew, and wished me well, "hope you get out of the shit," he said, but I was apprehensive.

"Freeborn!" an orderly barked, "the doctor is ready to see you now."

I'd been waiting there over an hour. I was a little nervous, but more curious as to what would happen. The doctor seemed polite; he introduced himself and questioned me as to what this inquiry was all about. After my rather lengthy and well-rehearsed explanation of why I was there, he looked down at a paper on his desk, and began speaking.

"The symptoms you are experiencing, in my opinion, have nothing to do with your blood disorder; are you getting enough sleep, are you eating well?", he inquired.

"No, not really," I responded.

We talked more, and the doctor made some guesses as why I might be feeling weak and tired. He mentioned parasites, blood-sucking insects and other nasty conditions that could be the cause of these symptoms. I got the feeling that this inquiry would not get me out of the bush, and I was right. A sense of calm seemed to come over me as I left the hospital, I would return to my squad and continue to hump the bush.

I flew back to Da Nang the next morning after some wait; I boarded a deuce and a half for the ride back to my Company area. Sitting at the back end of the truck I could see the open-front hootches, I could smell the diesel fuel and see the many roadside gas stations, which consisted of 3 or 4 one liter bottles of gasoline on small tables. The many motorized scooters and utility vehicles would gas up at these makeshift fueling stations. There were no gas stations as I knew them anywhere I traveled. I wondered what was to become of these people once we were gone. My thoughts were interrupted as the truck came to an abrupt stop, I was back home.

I checked in and the clerk told me to sit tight; I'd be going out with the next re-supply. I had a strange, easy feeling about that. I knew the squad needed me and I needed them; that's just the way it was.

Just before leaving Saigon, I wrote this letter.

December 3, 1971

Dear Dad,

Hi, how are you? I'm doing well. I'm in Saigon now, I've seen the doctor already, and he reports my health is good. He says my being tired does not relate to my operation. He said there is a possibility of my having a parasitic manifestation, whatever that is? He said it could be the reason I get tired out. I didn't know if they would check me for it, I really don't care. I want to get back to work. I had eight more months to do; I'd better get back on the ball.

I am going to take it easy here in Saigon. This is some place! They have traffic and people like any large city has. It's very different from Da Nang. It's more modernized than up north. They even drive our old 1957 Pontiacs and Chevys. There are a lot of older cars here. I'd say anywhere from 1948 to 1971. The 71's are owned mostly by the military, however. The Vietnamese still depend on motorbikes for their main mode of travel.

I'm staying at a place called the MACV compound. It's really nice. As a base, it's better than Fort Polk, Louisiana. It's hard to believe a place like this exists here in Nam. They have large stone office buildings, real nice living quarters, hot and cold showers. Right now I'm sitting on the sun deck of their Olympic size swimming pool. On the other side of the pool is a gym with all the equipment, including a tennis court. There is no war going on down here that's for sure. I haven't seen a bunker since I've been here, that sure seems strange.

Last night I went to the EM club and had filet mignon with mashed potatoes, all the goodies. It was delicious! The club itself was the nicest one I've seen since I've been in the Army. It really is unbelievable here.

I bought a nice little 35mm camera and I plan to get some good pictures of Saigon. That's what I'll be doing today. It's like being on vacation down here.

Well, I guess I'll end here. When I get back to Da Nang, I will get my flight home set up. I've got about 30 days, and then I'll really have it good, for a week or so, anyway.

Take care of yourself and say hello to everyone for me.

Love Joey

As promised, I had a little time and got the arrangements made for my trip home. It was getting real now. I would see my family once more, maybe the last time. My vision was very narrow these days, I lived moment to moment. I survived by shear will. I lived because I willed it, and God willed it. I was in His hands and as promised, everything would be all right.

December 8, 1971

Dear Dad,

Hi, how are you? I'm doing fine. I'm going back out today, as I am all through with the Congressional Inquiry. I guess they are sure I'm fine physically, so I guess that's that! On another note, I got some good news. I've completed my plans for my trip home. I purchased my ticket and I leave Vietnam 2 January at 12:45 PM. I'm due to arrive in San Francisco at 1400 hours on the same day. I have a four-hour delay there and I'm due in Newark airport at 0600 hours on 3 January. I decided it was best for all concerned that I take a bus from the Port Authority to Newburgh. I think that will be the most convenient way. I'm really looking forward to the trip home and the time off (from war). It'll sure be great seeing everyone again!

How's the weather? Have you gotten any more snow? I guess there will be plenty of snow to greet me. I sort of miss it you know. This is the first December I haven't seen any. Life sure is different for me now.

Well, I'll end here. Take care of yourself and if you got time, write.

Love Joey

I would finish the mission with the company; it was good to be back with my squad. They said they didn't miss me, but I knew that was bullshit. When it came time to bring rain down on the VC, nobody did it better than me. LT Clark commended me several times on my M-203 accuracy and skill. I had become proficient with the M-203 grenade launcher, and anyone on the receiving end of it was in a world of hurt.

Bob Hampel welcomed me back; he came over to my NDP and commented on how it wasn't the same out there without me. "And oh," Bob continued, "do you have an extra pound cake?"

We laughed, and I said "sure, but don't ask to borrow my toothbrush, cause I don't go that way."

Just havin' a little fun!

Chapter 14

In mid-December we rotated (returned) back to the rear area, but not totally without a mission. We were to take a few days off and then provide security (reactionary force) for our home base, Freedom Hill. This duty would be similar to that of China Beach, but we wouldn't have the South China Sea as a backdrop. The guard towers were manned 24 hours a day. We would work in 3-man teams, 12 hours shifts. One man would rest while the other 2 stood guard, rotating every 4 hours.

The Bob Hope USO Christmas Show was scheduled for December 21st at Freedom Hill. There was a large open area with a stage and plenty of room for spectators. Although stationed in different locations, the entire battalion would be there to see it. We got to stay in our regular Company area because we were on guard duty. At any rate we were all there to enjoy the show.

It was a rainy Tuesday afternoon as we made our way up to the show area. Freedom Hill provided many services for us; there was a PX, a commissary, a USO Club and other support facilities. If someone needed to call home, they could do it there. If they wanted to go on R&R, arrangements would be made there. It made life a little easier and normal for us.

The show was to start about 2:00 PM. We went early to get good seats up front. Most of my squad sat together on the ground, covered with our ponchos as the drizzle continued. Everyone seemed in good spirits, the Christmas spirit was alive and well. Finally, I saw Bob Hope's chopper set down behind the stage; I had a good view of him and his entourage as they got off the chopper. Bob was covered in some sort of poncho, not Army issue. He looked old and grey because he <u>was</u> old and grey in 1971. He started doing USO Christmas shows during WWII, then Korea, and now his 9th and next to last Christmas in Vietnam. It seemed surreal. It was exciting, and the crowd roared when they saw him. It was like a big party that day, despite the war and the rain.

After a while the show began, and of course "Thanks for the Memories" was played as Bob walked out on stage; the entire field erupted in cheers of appreciation. Bob Hope looked great, 20 years younger than just a few minutes ago. His hair was brown, slicked back the way he always wore it. He had his standard swagger and was carrying his trade mark golf club. He wore a 196th Infantry fatigue shirt, with our unit patch prominently displayed. It was like a scene from a Hollywood movie; I will never forget how he spent Christmas with us. He made his way around South Vietnam, bringing hope to us all. He thanked us for hanging around another year for him. He also wanted to know when the rain was going to stop; the place went wild with laughter. I never saw so many grunts laughing and having fun; I started to believe we might just get out of this thing; Bob was Hope for us all.

The next day, our last day off, the entire Company had a Christmas party. Guys had been getting packages from home for weeks and they were full of goodies. We set everything we had out on a large table and fired up our tape players and partied hardy.

December 15, 1971

Dear Dad,

Hi, how are you? I'm doing well. I received your letter today, and it was good hearing from you.

I think I failed to mention in my last letter that my stay in Saigon was brief. I stayed only two days, but I enjoyed myself. I'm back out in the bush, as the doctors are sure I'm enjoying good health. I'm feeling pretty good lately, maybe because I'm coming home.

I'm glad you decided not to send me any packages, as I'll have a lot to do when I go back to the rear, on 18 December. I usually have stuff I saved from packages, you know sort of reserve, but this takes baggage room. I'll have more than enough stuff to store away before I can leave. I will add anything you want to send when I return from my leave. It will be greatly appreciated. Packages mean a lot to one's morale.

I'm glad Uncle Harry is doing well. I'll visit him when I get home. I wrote him about two months ago but I guess they forgot about it.

Nothing much is happening over here. A few scares now and then. It keeps everyone on their toes. I'll have a lot to tell you when I get home. I'm sure Vietnam will be the main topic of my visit.

Well, I'd better end here, I probably won't write again before I get home. Take good care of yourself and say hi to everyone for me, even Tom. He never writes me, so he is number 10 on my list. Not really, but I'm disappointed. We'll see you in 17 days.

Love Joey

I wrote this letter while out in the bush after I returned from Saigon. It would be my last letter from

Nam as I would be going home soon and there wouldn't be much time to write.

The reactionary force lasted until December 27th and then we headed back out to the bush. LZ Maude was our next AO, a remote clearing used as tactical air support for gunships, troop deployment, supplies, etc. This base would come under fire from time to time and needed constant security. The terrain was rugged with many small villages. That usually meant lots of VC as they used these vills as cover. Our mission was to sweep the AO for explosives, mortars, booby traps and other undesirable shit the VC would leave for us.

This remote outpost was not usually manned, but there were always grunts around keeping it secure. There were many LZs in Nam, but by now more and more were being shut down. Maude would not be around much longer, it was our last time there.

I was told I'd be extracted from the bush on January 1st, as a re-supply was scheduled for that day. That only gave me 2 days in the rear to get myself ready to go. I had a lot to do and tried to get my thoughts together. I had many concerns. My safety was one and getting out of the bush was another. I'd be heading back to the world soon, I couldn't wait.

The area around Maude was marshy, lots of rice paddies and other agricultural crops. There were a lot of mustard plants which grew into very large bushes. What they did with them was a mystery to me.

There were several water buffalos (cows) around, which were used exclusively as beasts of burden. The cows were tangible signs of wealth and prosperity and regarded as sacred.

Occasionally we would happen upon a village, the rules at that time were to be respectful to the civilians. We would never enter a village without being invited by the chieftain. Once inside, we would visually inspect for signs of VC, weapons or munitions. They knew why we were there. If we were not welcomed, we would become suspicious and report that to CP, then move on.

My day had finally come, January 1st, 1972. New Year's Day was just another day out in the bush. We would get re-supplied, and I would return with the re-supply team. I had to start thinking like a civilian. My grunt language had to be checked, in Nam we had our own way of talking to each other. Sometimes I would catch myself using grunt lingo while I was home.

As the helicopter off loaded the re-supply, Speed came by to wish me well.

"No big deal, I'll be back in 2 weeks Speed, take care," I told him.

He was planning an in-country R&R soon. We said goodbye, and I made my way to the chopper, jumped on; I was going home. I got a letter on that re-supply; I stuffed it in my shirt pocket, I would read it on the way in. The chopper began to whine, and soon we were airborne.

December 15, 1971

Hi Joey,

We just got your letter dated December 8, and I'm hoping this will reach you in time, before you leave. We were unhappy to hear nothing came of the exam, and that you had to go back to the "bush", but I'm glad to hear you arranged for the leave and we'll be waiting for you on January 3.

We had a little wet snow last night, but it didn't amount to much, it turned warm and has been raining on and off all day.

We are all okay and I'm working nights for the next two weeks so I should be good and tired by Christmas Eve.

Tom can't write, the best he can do is watch the boob tube, and at this he is an expert. I suppose he's not feeling too well and we are going to find out if he will need the operation you had, but we'll discuss this when we see you.

Take good care, have a good Christmas.

See you soon. Love Dad

On December 15, 1971, Hamilton Fish Jr. wrote a letter addressed to my Dad. It read he was pleased to submit the report from the Department of the Army showing the results of a previous examination. He said he appreciated the opportunity to look into this matter and hoped that my Dad will find the information to be satisfactory.

The official report as received by Hamilton Fish and sent to my Dad, read in part as follows:

THIS IS IN REPLY TO YOUR INQUIRY CONCERNING SPECIALIST FOUR

JOSEPH FREEBORN

SPECIALIST FREEBORN HAS BEEN EXAMINIED BY A HEMATOLOGIST CONCERNING

HIS HEREDITARY SPHEROCYBOSIS, AT THE 3RD FIELD HOSPITAL, SIAGON, REPUBLIC OF VIETNAM. THE

EXAMINATION REVEALED THAT HIS RED BLOOD CELL COUNT WAS NORMAL AND THAT HIS WHITE BLOOD CELL COUNT INCREASED FROM THE AMOUNT SHOWN DURING A PREVIOUS EXAMINATION. HE HAS BEEN REFERRED TO HIS BATTALION SURGEON FOR CONTINUED OBSERVATION WITH RESPECT TO THE WHITE CELL COUNT. SPECIALIST FREEBORN IS CONSIDERED FIT FOR DUTY IN THE REPUBLIC OF VIETNAM.

The report said I enjoyed a high state of morale and I was scheduled to complete my tour of duty on or about July 31, 1972. My Dad never shared this letter with me while I was in Nam. Only after I returned home did he show me the letter and report.

Chapter 15

I had my orders! I stuffed my duffle bag with everything I needed while on R&R; my level of excitement was building. I would be transported to Saigon, via C-130 standby. I got on the first C-130 transport out; the flight was uneventful. Once I arrived at Tan Son Nhut Airport, Saigon, I was directed to the commercial terminal, a short walk from the military arrivals terminal. I noticed a flurry of activity as I made my way down the walkway. Suddenly there it was, the biggest, most beautiful airplane I had ever seen. It was a glistening Pan-Am 747 Jumbo Jet, with the "World" written all over it. Soon I would be seated and on my way home. It was such a drastic contrast to where I had just been--the bush.

The large waiting area was crowded; everyone would be boarding this "Freedom Bird". I spotted MPs carrying M-16s on security detail, which reminded me where I was. There were many uniformed military personnel, most were older than me and they definitely out ranked me. I wondered who the civilians were; perhaps reporters or non-military contractors.

To say I was a little nervous as I boarded the Jumbo Jet would have been an understatement. I had only flown three times in my life and didn't know how something so huge could stay airborne. I found my assigned seat and settled in. The Jumbo Jet had 3 seats, 5 seats and 3 seats, per row. I was lucky; they assigned me an aisle seat in the 5 seat section in the middle of the plane. My view of the large movie screen was unobstructed, and I had plenty of leg room. Still, I couldn't believe I was going home; it was dreamlike and very unsettling.

I'd left my squad out in the bush, one man short. They gave my grenadier duties (M-203) to another guy who had no experience with the weapon. In Nam we depended on each other for our survival. Each man had his job to do when things got hairy. This contributed to the uneasy feeling I had all the time I was home.

The flight was long, about 23 hours. It was morning, then evening, and then morning again. The meal schedule was unpredictable, and it seemed I was eating breakfast every other meal. I think they determined the meals by the setting and rising of the sun. Once you cross the International Dateline, days are lost or gained depending on direction of travel.

I slept a lot along the way and when I was awake, I could not shake the feeling of desertion. Yes, I was going home, but my attention and senses were still in Nam. I had to get over it, once home things might be better.

We landed mid-morning on January 3rd at Newark Airport. I had asked my family not to meet me at the airport, but was overruled. They were there waiting for me. As I made my way down the arrivals ramp, I caught sight of Angie first, then my sister and my Dad. We briefly greeted each other and continued walking to the baggage claim area. There were lots of hugs, kisses and just good feelings as we waited for my duffle bag to show up. I was dressed in civilian clothes; they felt uncomfortable. I also had my dress uniform for the return trip, 1 dress shirt, shoes and OD (olive drab) green underwear. I left all my field gear and personal stuff in a locker in the rear area; I could not take anything war related home.

We talked all the way home; I was getting filled in on all that was going on. I noticed the conversation was light-hearted and Nam was never mentioned. I never thought I would return home and I had made my peace with eminent death. Vietnam had a way of dispelling any hope for the future; it was survival for the here and now. I had to pinch myself as I sat close to Angie in the back seat. I never stopped touching her, it seemed dream-like. We were getting to know each other again after almost 6 months separated.

She had to be uncomfortable, but she never let on; I know I was. Soon we would be together alone, I couldn't wait.

The visit home included a whirlwind of events and get-togethers to the point of exhaustion. I would lie in my bed at home and imagine this whole Vietnam thing was just a bad dream, and I would wake up and go on with the rest of my life. At times I would wake suddenly, thinking I was in Nam. There were thoughts of going to Canada and sitting out this war, but my brothers in Nam were waiting for me to return. I ran the full gamut of emotions and feelings during my time home. I was glad for this time to think, relax and feel all the love I had there.

I took lots of pictures, my home, my car, my family, my girlfriend, and took them back with me. It helped keep this R&R alive after I returned. They would often get me through tough times.

My two week R&R was ending, I was leaving the next day. I planned to catch the Short Line bus to New York Port Authority, and then a bus to JFK Airport. My return flight was out of Terminal One where Pan American Airlines had a huge presence. The best flights were out of JFK, with one short layover in Hawaii. I picked that flight because I always wanted to see Hawaii.

The goodbyes started a few days before I was to leave, first my friends, then my family and finally, the hardest goodbye was with Angie. I could see she was trying to be strong and not show her despair, but it was thinly masked. I was convinced I would not be returning; it was a long shot at best. I never conveyed this to anyone, but these feelings were strong. As the time passed in Vietnam, I couldn't quite shake these thoughts; it went with the hopeless territory we occupied.

Angie had waited for me these 6 months; she never dated anyone and seemed willing to wait another 6 months or more. I had a 2 year hitch and hadn't completed 10 months yet. I wanted to tell her not to wait, but I knew she wouldn't have it and neither would I. We loved each other, as best a young couple could. We discussed marriage and a future together, but I still wasn't sure I'd be coming home.

I boarded the Pan Am 747 about 4:30 PM and it took about an hour for everyone to board the plane, after all it held over 500 people. The flight was packed, with most people going to Honolulu. I was looking forward to seeing the Big Island. I would be there for four hours.

In Hawaii, we boarded another 747 and headed to Guam, where we would drop off and take on new passengers. We did not have to disembark, just sit tight for about 40 minutes. I ordered another drink just before they stowed the bar cart and it helped make the wait more tolerable.

A young lady boarded the flight in Hawaii, she sat in the window seat and I was in the aisle, no one sat in the middle. We talked most of the way to Guam. She was to catch another flight to New Zealand where she lived. I found our discussions very interesting and made the trip go quickly. The subject of Vietnam seemed to be the major topic and she could not understand why I was going back. At one point she offered me the opportunity to go to New Zealand with her so I wouldn't have to go back. The idea seemed crazy, but it flattered me that she would even consider such a thing. No, I told her I had brothers waiting for me; they too want to go on leave. I thought of her offer long after I returned.

The Jumbo Jet set down in Da Nang this time, not Saigon. I only had a short ride back to the rear area. We loaded into a deuce and a half and made our way down the winding roadway to different company areas. We made several stops and guys piled out. I was the last guy to get off.

I arrived at my company area and checked in with the new Company Clerk.

"Hi, I'm Joe Freeborn coming back from R&R," I announced.

"Don (Don Williams) is my name, welcome back," he said jokingly.

"Yeah, great to be back," I replied, we laughed.

He was a new replacement, just got in-country and was waiting for permanent assignment.

"The Company is out in the bush, not sure where. You need to get squared away ASAP, you'll be going out tomorrow morning with a re-supply," Don instructed.

Hmm, I thought, just like 2 weeks ago. Don't mean nothin'; I was back and anxious to reunite with the guys.

"I'll have my shit together, Don, no sweat," I confidently replied.

I spent the rest of the afternoon getting my stuff put together. I was glad to see all my gear was still in the locker and I had my things back in my possession. We became dependent on our gear, it was personal to us.

Bird-in-bound, someone shouted, the re-supply was waiting on the LZ. We all joined in and loaded the stuff on the chopper. There was a little room for me to squeeze in and off we went. I studied the terrain, the rice paddies, the villages, the water buffalo, all the smells and sights seemed all too familiar, I was home again; the war was still on, nothing had changed, not even me.

They greeted me with hey, Freeborn, where ya been? Sand bagging somewhere, yeah, getting over like a fat rat! They laughed, and it all seemed familiar.

The squad was in tack, but I noticed a few new faces. I asked Bob, "Who are they?"

"Newbies," he replied, "they got here last re-supply. We needed replacements, some of the older guys left."

Newbies were dangerous; they didn't know shit from Shinola. I was at once concerned and on guard.

"Are they squared away?" I asked.

"Yeah, they're getting their shit together; this one guy, Rocky (Rocky Thurman), I've taken as my assistant pig gunner, he's cool," Bob reported.

"Great," I replied. "What happened to Terry?"

"Reassigned to CP, he's humpin' a radio now, I've got the pig," Bob proudly announced.

"Cool."

It didn't take long; I was humping again, and we were getting ready to set up our NDP for the night. The heat felt strange and I was a little tired, but I was back, doing my thing in Nam, trying to stay alive.

We patrolled an area around Firebase Linda, not much was happening, just the way we liked it. We were going back in soon and then to the ridgeline for about 2 weeks, pulling security. The ridgeline was a series of small mountains overlooking the airfield in Da Nang. It was easy duty, almost tolerable.

No letters yet, I thought, as it took 2-3 weeks for letters to arrive and I had only been back 2 weeks. I had written everyone at least once by now and was waiting for a reply.

"Hey Sarg, any letters for me?" I shouted.

"Nope, too bad," he shot back.

We made our way to the ridgeline; it was bare dirt mounds with small sand bag hootches strewn over the entire area. There was a CP in the center of the fortified bunkers and a Loch chopper pad. A Loch was a small 2 man helicopter and its actual name was Low Flying Observation Helicopter. They would come and go all day. I always wanted to take a ride, but that never happened.

When on the ridgeline, the local kids would sneak up to visit us. It was the only time I came in direct contact with Vietnamese civilians. They lived at the base of the ridgeline and had a well-beaten trail up to the ridge. They would sell us stuff and were friendly. Some could even speak a little English; they picked it up by listening to the others who occupied the ridge. I was a little guarded when they were around and never turned my back on them, well almost never.

One day I was cleaning myself up, washing, brushing teeth, etc., when a bunch of them showed up at my bunker. They were just hanging around and I was busy getting dressed. I had taken off a beautiful heavy 18K gold chain my girlfriend Angie had given me when I was home. When I arrived in Nam, Angie was in Italy, near Vicenza (known for its gold jewelry). She bought the chain for me and was going to keep it until I came home for good. I asked if I could have it sooner, so she gave it to me while on leave.

Suddenly, I thought about the chain; I had hung it on a nail outside the entrance to the bunker. I went to get it, it was gone, and so were the kids. Oh shit, now what I wondered? I'll never see that again and was sick over losing it.

The next day, one of the kids who visited me the day before happened to walk by.

"Hey Jimmy," his GI assigned nick name, "come over here," I called out.

I told him my chain was missing and in his limited English he swore he knew nothing about it. Out of desperation, I told him I would pay $20 US dollars to get it back.

"I try, I try, see you tomorrow, I try," he said, as he made his way down the trail.

Later that afternoon Jimmy returned with my chain. I took the chain and threatened him within an inch of his life if I ever saw him or his buddies up here again. He ran away, and I never saw any of them again. I kept the $20 bill and slept with one eye open the rest of my time there.

Chapter 16

The weather was getting warmer and more humid; monsoon season was ending as it only rained occasionally now. We were coming in off the ridgeline for Reactionary Force Security. We'd be in the rear for 5 to 6 days providing security for our rear area. Guard duty would be our only task.

Some guys were going to Bangkok for R&R now that we had the replacements on board. The newbies, having spent time out in the bush, seemed ok. The Company needed to regroup and get some rest. There would be time for movies, EM club fun, and just kickin' back. Of course there would be plenty of pot smoking with music blaring.

I was still thinking of my visit home. I recalled everything I did and experienced; I missed home and wanted to go back, but that wasn't happening.

I resigned myself to keeping it together, being careful and getting this over with as best I could.

Things had changed when I returned from R&R. The whole vibe felt different. We had a new Company

Clerk, Sgt. Don Wilkens. We had a new 1st Sergeant (Tilden Robinson), a new Company Commander (Daniel Cleary) and a couple of new 2nd Lieutenants.

Many of the older guys had rotated back to the States, and we had 9 new replacements. These replacements would be the last we would get here in Nam, although I did not know that at the time. I had heard rumors that our unit was going to stand down; that is leave Vietnam and return to the States. There were no schedules or plans, just rumors.

I was now one of the old guys, a seasoned grunt having spent over 7 months in-country. A lot had happened in the two short weeks I was home; things here were very dynamic.

February 16, 1972

Hi Joey,

I first got your letter yesterday; I didn't know what was going on. I thought maybe you were on your way to Hawaii. But I'm glad to hear the news that maybe it won't be too long, The Birds (B-52 Bombers) *have been trying to break up any large build-up of the VC and I think they have succeeded.*

(He was referring to the beginning of "Operation Linebacker II").

I wrote a couple of times before and you probably have them by now, everything is okay here, Suzanne is leaving for the Islands for a week and I'll be having my vacation at the same time, so I'll try to get some things done around here, we still have no snow and the weather is mild during the day, the road is a little muddy at times but nothing like the big thaw we've had.

As I wrote in the last letter 3 payments will be made on the car now and leaves 4 more which will be paid in 2 months so that's not too bad.

I'll try to get Tom to write again, that's as hard as pulling teeth, but once he gets the habit of it I'm sure it won't be so bad. I'm glad you enjoyed his letter.

I had the day off today and spent it washing clothes and floors and defrosted the freezer, and I'm tired, this housework in no joke.

I'll close for now hoping all is well and I'll write again soon, watch for the package.

Love Dad

This was the first letter from Dad since returning from R&R, the others he mentioned never arrived. While up on the ridgeline I wrote a few letters. Here is one to Dad.

February 26, 1972

Dear Dad,

Hi, how are you? I'm doing well. I received your letter dated the 16th a few days ago. I got the package from Aunt Pauline about the same time. She sent it for St. Valentine's Day, that was nice of her, wasn't it?

You mentioned the B-52 strikes that have been going on over here lately. Well, they have been really effective, as far as breaking up NVA concentrations, they don't have much to give us, and we're doing a job on the little they have. I guess the protesters are really screaming. Nevertheless, we're doing a good job on stopping ground offensives

I'm definitely "short"; my days over here are numbered. I figure if I'm still here in April, something is wrong.

I heard on the news a few days ago the Eastern coast got quite a severe snowstorm. Did you get any of it?

There really isn't too much happening here. I'm up on this ridgeline pulling security for Da Nang. We'll be out here until the 3rd of March. Then we go in the rear after this as a reactionary force to insure the Military Installation remains safe. It's easy. I've heard rumors we'll be standing down soon after that. We'll see. Love, Joey

December 3, 1971

Nixon orders the initiation of Operation Linebacker II

The Nixon administration announces that the bombing and mining of North Vietnam will resume and continue until a "settlement" is reached.

On December 13, North Vietnamese negotiators walked out of secret talks with National Security Advisor Henry Kissinger. President Richard Nixon issued an ultimatum to Hanoi to send its representatives back to the conference table within 72 hours "or else". The North Vietnamese rejected Nixon's demand, and the President ordered Operation Linebacker II, a full-scale air campaign against the Hanoi area. White House Press Secretary Ronald Ziegler said the bombing would end only if all U.S. prisoners of war were released and an internationally recognized cease-fire was in force.

Linebacker II was the most concentrated air offensive of the war, and was conducted by U.S. aircraft, including B-52s, Air Force fighter-bombers flying from bases in Thailand, and Navy and Marine fighter-bombers flying from carriers in the South China Sea. During the 11 days of the attack, we flew 700 B-52 sorties and over 1,000 fighter-bomber sorties. These planes dropped roughly 20,000 tons of bombs, mostly over the densely populated area between Hanoi and Haiphong.

The North Vietnamese fired over 1,000 surface-to-air missiles at the attacking aircraft and also used their MiG fighter-interceptor squadrons, eight MiG's were shot down. In a throwback to past aerial combat, Staff Sgt. Samuel O. Turner, the tail gunner on a Boeing B-52D bomber, downed a trailing MiG-21 with a blast from his 50-caliber machine gun over Hanoi. Six days later, airman, first class Albert E. Moore, also a B-52 gunner, shot down a second MiG-21 after a strike on the Thai Nguyen rail yard. These were the only aerial gunner kills of the war. We lost twenty-six U.S. aircraft, including 15 B-52s. Three aircraft were brought down by MiGs; the rest, including the B-52s, were downed by surface-to-air missiles.

American antiwar activists dubbed Linebacker II the "Christmas bombing", and charged that it involved "carpet bombs" deliberately targeting civilian areas with intensive bombing that "carpeted" a city with bombs. The campaign was focused on specific military targets and was not intended to be "carpet bombing", but it resulted in the deaths of 1,318 civilians in Hanoi.

We deemed the Linebacker II bombing a success because in its wake, the North Vietnamese returned to the negotiating table, where the Paris Peace Accords were signed less than a month later.

March 2, 1972

Dear Dad,

Hi, how are you? I'm doing fine. Hope this letter finds everyone well. I'm writing to tell you I sent a camera and a camera kit home the other day. They will be in separate packages. (2) When you receive them let me know, and open them up, or rather you can open them up, but don't lose the instruction pamphlets as I need them to learn how to operate the camera, and with some care, it'll last a long time. I figure a camera is a nice thing to have, as time goes so quickly, and pictures sort of prolong good memories. So be expecting the parcels, Ok?

There isn't much news on my end, or rather, this side of the world. I've been following Pres. Nixon's trip to

China, by way of the radio, and it seems his trip turned out ok. UPI news interviewed me while we were up on Firebase Linda; maybe you saw my comments on his trip in the New York Times, or maybe even my picture. I was writing Christine (my cousin) a letter at the time. This reporter came up to me and asked what I thought of Nixon's trip. I told him I thought the trip wouldn't amount to much, and that I dis-trusted oriental people as far as any verbal agreement might go. There was an article in our daily paper, The Stars & Stripes, and the headline caption read "G.I. Cast Cautious Eye on President's Trip." As a whole, the article was pessimistic, as far as accomplishing any settlement over here. That's the main thoughts of all of us here in Nam. Nevertheless, it proves that all Americans are not war-crazy, as so many people of the world believe. It also shows the North Vietnamese we want peace, but can't get it.

My part here is almost over. The unit isn't standing down too soon, but they are giving drops, for those whose DEROS (Date Expected to Return from Overseas) date is in July. The drops so far are up to July 29, my DEROS date is July 31. I'll be getting the next drop. People who DEROS anytime from now through July 29 will leave March 17, 1972. I missed those dates by 2 days. I'll probably get out in April, I think. It'll be better than nothing.

Well, I'll end here. I'll be sending the check soon. I go in to the rear tomorrow, so I'll do it sometime in the near future. Be expecting the camera, keep it safe. Bye for now.

Love Joey

PS. I may make Sergeant soon.

Chapter 17

I was walking to the mess hall one day and noticed an announcement, looking for S4 Supply help. Some of the jobs listed were clerk typist, office helper, Jeep drivers, couriers, truck drivers, etc. I noted the meeting would be later that day, so I decided to check it out. I never knew the Army posted job positions as we all had specific MOS's or occupations. Mine was 11B20 Infantry. I arrived at the S4 building and joined a group of guys who already started to assemble. I didn't know anyone; I had seen a few guys around, probably from other companies in my Battalion. An officer came out eventually and explained these positions were being filled based on experience, there was no training cycle provided. You would be temporarily reassigned to S4 from your unit if approved by your Company Commander. I know some of you are grunts, and may not qualify.

I listened intently as he barked out the jobs available. "I need a truck driver who has a military driver's license," the officer shouted.

"I do," someone replied.

"See Sgt. Miller over there." Then he would yell out another job and someone else would respond.

This went on for a while, and then it finally came, "Who Knows How to Type?" the officer shouted.

"I do," I said.

"See the sergeant," was his reply.

Now, I had taken a ½ semester of typing in high school because I needed an elective and the class was full of cute girls. I had no intention of doing any real typing. I was also shocked that I volunteered for this rear job.

I was a grunt; I belong out in the bush where things were more familiar. Mortar and sapper attacks rarely happen out in the bush. What was I doing? Had I finally lost my way, I wondered?

"How many words a minute can you type soldier?" the sergeant asked.

"Sixty or so," I replied. I was lying; I had tested about 40-45 wpm tops.

"What's your MOS?" he asked.

"11B20," I replied.

"What company?"

"Bravo," I said.

"Ok, here's the scoop, you take this form, sign it and have your CO approve it and get it back to me ASAP, ok?" he continued.

"I'll do it right away," and headed back to my Company area.

I had enough of being a grunt; the squad had changed, my level of confidence was waning, and this might be just what I needed to survive this war. Maybe it was divine intervention, I didn't know. I walked into the CO's office and requested to see him.

"Wait here," Don said, and then he shouted, "come on in Freeborn."

I stood in front of the Captain's desk, saluted and stood at attention.

"At ease," he said, "what's going on?" Capt. Cleary asked.

"I have this request for temporary duty assignment from S4 Supply," I replied, as I handed it to him.

He looked up, took the form and glanced at it quickly. "What's the matter, you want out of the bush?" he asked.

"Yes," I said, "I'd like to try something else for a while, it's only temporary," I mumbled.

"Let me look it over, I'll get back to you," he said dismissively. I thanked him and left.

I was feeling like a deserter again, like I did when I was on R&R, the same feeling washed over me. I made my way to the EM Club; I needed a beer.

The next day the Company Clerk stopped me, "the CO is looking for you, better make tracks, chop chop." The office was a flurry of activity; it seemed every squad leader and platoon leader was finishing up a meeting. I walked in and took a seat on a bench. A few minutes later, the Clerk came in.

"Hey Freeborn, did the Old Man see you yet?"

"No," I replied.

"Wait, I'll see what he's doing."

"He'll see you now," Don said. I went right in.

"Ok," Capt. Cleary said, "I have discussed this with LT Clarke and in his opinion I should let you give this a try. I'm not so enthused. We have a bunch of newbies out there and I need experienced guys like you. LT Clarke feels he can cover your ass for a while, but we may need you back out in the bush."

I agreed.

"You've got the new job Freeborn," he continued, "I'm only here a few weeks, but you have a good record, you've got your shit together. LT wants to put you up for a hard 5 (sergeant) promotion, but this new assignment will delay the promotion. You need more combat time before I can recommend you for E-5. I will have you back in this unit if the need should arise. That's it, good luck."

I thanked him, saluted and left his office. Now I was really sick, hard 5 I thought, if I had only known, I never would have volunteered for this stupid clerk typist job. I did it; I had no other option now. I really f... up this time, I thought.

I was kind of in limbo for the next day or two; the guys were getting ready to go back out, and I didn't know what I was to do.

"Wait for your new orders," Don instructed, "they are being cut now over at Headquarters. When I get them, you will officially be assigned. You will not physically go anywhere, as you are still loosely assigned to Bravo Company, just a different job. That's what the Old Man wants. Captain told me if we needed you out in the bush you'd be able to get out there faster by having you nearby. I have a hootch assigned for you across the walkway, next to the armory. You have a bunk, footlocker, and a small fridge left by the last guy who occupied that hootch. Go to quartermaster and pull your bedding, towels, and 7 new sets of fatigues and new boots. Get your name sewn on them, people need to see your name, we all have them."

He showed me his clean green fatigue shirt with Wilkens printed on the name tag.

"You also need your rank. No ribbons or shit like that. Oh, your hootch maid's name is Rosie, she gets a few bucks a week from all the guys in that hootch. She cleans up after you and does your laundry. I'll get back to you when the orders come in."

"Thanks," I said, and went back to the barracks.

I had to break the news to the squad. I collared Festus, my squad leader, and he already knew.

"LT told me yesterday," he grinned, "you'll be getting over, you lucky fu...er." We laughed.

"Does everyone else know?" I asked.

"I think so, don't mean nothing," he said.

In other words, it didn't matter. Guys come and go all the time, I was no exception.

The next morning the Company was to be airlifted out, about 10:00 AM. I walked down to the chopper pad with them as I had done many times before. We joked around; they made fun of me, calling me names like pussy, shit head, REMP (Rear Escalon Military Personnel). That is what I was now. We always held REMPs in contempt; they were bored, used drugs, and lied about what they were doing over here in letters they mailed home. We always made fun of them, justified or not, that's what we'd do. I saw them off and walked back to the Company area; I felt bad and had a tremendous feeling of loss. What was I going to do I wondered, I can't type!

I bumped into Don at breakfast. "Your orders are here, pick them up after chow, and report to a Sgt. Smithe over at S4," he informed me.

Immediately my stomach began to churn and hurt. I didn't have my new clothes and boots and such. "What about my clothes Don?" I asked.

"Don't sweat it, you're in the rear now, things take time. Stop by later."

I picked up the paperwork, all signed and sealed. It was official; I was a clerk typist according to the orders. My name was just one of many, recalling all the positions S4 had to fill. I made my way across the compound to the large metal supply building.

"I'm looking for Sgt. Smithe," I said.

"He's in there," the PFC pointed to a door. "Go on in," he directed. I walked in and took a seat.

"Where's your orders?" Smithe asked. I handed them to him. "Ok see you tomorrow at 0800 hours," he curtly responded.

I left and got my stuff together and settle into my hootch. It took most of the day.

The fatigues were stiff and new, the boots black and uncomfortable; I felt like a newbie and hated the feeling. I got my headgear and a few other items and reported to S4 as instructed.

"You'll sit here at this desk," Smithe told me.

It was a gray metal desk with a wooden squeaky chair. Atop the desk sat an old black manual typewriter, the ones with the off white round keys. I had only typed on an electric typewriter, but I had seen these typewriters before. My mother was a Teletype Operator for Western Union, and she could sure type fast on one of those typewriters. I sat there for a while collecting my thoughts, when suddenly someone gave me a form to fill out.

"Type it," the clerk said.

It was an informational form about me, so I went to work, picking and pecking.

I worked in the office for a few weeks; I was getting used to the routine and the workload was a joke, there wasn't any. I used to come in late, go to chow early, come back late, no one cared. Remember, we were in Nam. No one cared. These guys have been getting over; now, so was I.

"Freeborn, can you drive?" Smithe asked.

"Sure," I said, I even have a military driver's license.

"Good, let's go."

I followed him outside and there was a brand new military Jeep parked. The Major needs a Jeep driver, and all the regular guys are out. He needs to go over to Gunfighter Village (as we called it), a small village a few clicks from here.

"When?" I asked.

"Soon, sit tight." I went back to my desk and waited.

Some time passed and Major Keene came out of his office. "Who's driving me?" he asked Smithe.

"Freeborn over there," he replied.

"Ok, I'll be back in a few," he reported. We walked out of the office and I started the Jeep.

"Do you know the way?" Major Keene asked.

"No sir," I replied.

"I'll show you."

This was the first time I drove a vehicle in Nam, on roads I never traveled, to a village I had never seen. I handled it well I thought, and I enjoyed getting out of the stuffy office. The Major was a regular guy; we never displayed rank when out of the company area. He did not show any, and my rank didn't matter. I felt at ease with him and he seemed to be ok with me. We got back a few hours later; he thanked me for the ride.

"Leave the Jeep," Smithe instructed, "I'll pull into the motor pool later, see ya tomorrow."

I would drive the Major from time to time and looked forward to it. The typing job was a piece of cake, and I was getting comfortable living in the rear. The Company was coming in soon, and I didn't seem to envy them anymore. I knew they would be dirty, smelly and tired. They would pull guard duty on Firebase Linda, and that was always a boring stint. I had been there, and it sucked. I was glad I wasn't going with them; yep, I was settlin' in.

It was mid-March now and the rumor mill was working overtime. We were standing down, Nixon would pull troops and the 1st/46th was on the short list to leave. When and where, no one knew. Washington, DC didn't even know.

Finally, a list came out. It stated if you came in country before Sept 1, 1971, you would be eligible for the "Early Phasedown Release Program". That was me; I came here August 3, 1971, I might be leaving this shit hole soon. Information was not forthcoming immediately, but little by little facts emerged. Then orders were cut and finally I was on the list; I had a DEROS (Date Expected to Return from Over Seas) date. My long nightmare was almost over, but, stay tuned, there is more to come.

Chapter 18

I was driving the Headquarters Jeep more these days; I think they finally realized I couldn't type. No one ever said anything, but I suspect that's the reason. I had ventured further and further away from Freedom Hill (our rear area) and was getting a better insight on how backwards and even primitive this country really was. Earlier in my tour, I saw devastating poverty in Cam Rahn Bay, but now it was close up. They lived in open front shed-like structures, cobbled together with scrap materials, salvaged or stolen from us. The floors were dirt or corrugated steel, the kind we used for chopper LZs. They usually cooked outside, and the smells were sometimes unbearable, at least to me. Their diet consisted mostly of home-grown vegetables, lots of rice and fish heads, and other discarded parts from the fishermen's catch. They reportedly ate cats, dogs and even rats, which were once plentiful there. I never saw one cat all the time I was in Nam, so I assumed cats were on the menu. The average annual wage was $400 for the Vietnam people.

I kept checking the bulletin board and day after day I was disappointed. Apparently they slowed down the exodus from Vietnam as command was reporting heavier than normal VC activity. Sapper attacks were on the rise and the fire base we supported (Linda) had been mortared and breached. We had reduced troop strength, and the VC knew it; they seemed to know everything.

Finally, the day came, there it was: FREEBORN, JOSEPH A. 083436223 printed on the DEROS (Date Expected to Return from Over Seas) list. My orders to leave this hell hole would come soon. I was so excited! I ran over to Headquarters Company and asked one of the administrative sergeants, "when are my orders going to come through Sarg?"

"I don't know," he barked, "you'll have to wait. Your CO from Company B will get them and he will notify you in due time," he continued.

Captain Cleary, I hadn't thought of him in a while. I immediately made it over to the old Company area, walked into the CO's office and inquired about my orders.

"Not yet, the list just came out," the clerk replied. "You lucked out, command has been cutting back on DEROS dates, shits hittin' the fan out there, in case you didn't know. I'll see if there is anything in the afternoon communications from the higher ups and let you know, come by later."

I didn't feel lucky, however; I was still stuck here with no orders. I would remain guardedly optimistic until I had the orders in hand.

I waited day after day, checking with the Company Clerk, the answer was always the same.

"Not yet, keep checking in," he told me.

The wait was difficult, I had a lot of things to do before I could leave here, and I was getting anxious. My mind would wander and staying focused was becoming more difficult. I wanted to go home, and I was really "short". Too short I thought.

I was checking with HHC (Headquarters Company) for my daily trip log and anything else they needed me to do.

"Hey Freeborn," Smithe shouted, "get your ass over to B Company they need to see you TT."

I dropped everything and made tracks over to B Company. As I literally ran over to B Company, I knew the orders had finally landed and my date to leave would be printed right there in plain sight. Don met me; he informed me they needed me out on Fire Base Linda.

"What?" I questioned.

"Yeah, they're short grunts out there." I thought I was done with that, my mind was racing.

"The old man wants you to go over to S4 Supply and get your field gear reissued." Don continued.

"What happened out there?" I inquired.

"Don't know exactly, your squad needs more guys and you're up."

"Shit," I mumbled. I wasn't ready for this, I was going home soon. "How about my orders?" I asked.

"Forget that," Don immediately replied, "you'll be here for a while, so get goin'. You'll be movin' out tomorrow morning."

I was numb; I was so short and now my DEROS would to be undetermined. I still had over 4 months left on my tour of duty and Capt. Cleary had told me I was only on loan to HHC Company. I stumbled back over to S4 in total disbelief this was happening. I knew the most dangerous time in Nam was when you were short. Your attention to details, like fighting a war, was second to going home. I had just spent several weeks pumping myself up, and now I was totally deflated. I got to the warehouse and drew all my gear. It was all there just like I left it; even my old nasty well-worn boots, everything. I couldn't help from thinking; they probably knew I would need this stuff again.

I brought my field gear back to my hootch and found some mail on my bunk. Having a permanent residence meant no more mail calls; the Company Clerk would deliver letters and packages as they came into his office. I quickly tore open the letter from Dad; I needed to get a dose of his lightheartedness. He always wrote uplifting letters, and they made me feel better somehow. I needed a dose of his optimism right now.

March 20, 1972
Hi Joey,

We got two letters from you in the past couple of days one dated March 12th and the other March 14th. I'm glad you're in a position now that you can at least write in peace and have some time to yourself.

From the news we get here, things are quiet over there. The only incident we heard of was a mortar attack on a firebase around Da Nang and a few attacks at

Saigon. The plane attacks (Operation Rolling Thunder) have seemed to be effective in keeping them off balance and I hope destroying their supplies and whatnot. I'm hoping that things are slowing down a little.

The politicians are going at it hot and heavy and this guy (George) Wallace made a good showing in the primaries in Florida. He got 48% of the vote and (John) Lindsay got 7%

They say that he is a dangerous man because he wants to bring back sanity to the nation, and I suppose in this age we're in, this notion can't be too popular, but he stands for all the things that made this nation what it had been before the bleeding heart bums started crying on everyone's shoulder.

He won mostly on the anti-bussing question and a few days after his victory, Pres. Nixon came on the TV and said the same thing he did. Lindsay and his stooges were for this, plus amnesty for draft dodgers, deserters etc. and he was badly beaten, so there must be some sane people left in Florida. Let's hope so!

The only problem we had with the snow was that the Ford (1941 Ford 9N tractor) wasn't in operation otherwise we would have had it made. It's been laid up all winter, I didn't have the time to work on it but from now on I will; the road is pretty messy right now and they predict rain tonight and tomorrow, so I guess this will be the worst of it. We barely made it home tonight, the ruts are really deep but I'll be home tomorrow, Wednesday, and I hope to be able to do something to help the situation, but you know how it gets, the only thing to cure it is to get the snow off those banks and from then on we're on easy street. But we do need a good vehicle to move the snow and kind of smooth things over, I was thinking along the same lines, so when you get home we'll look around for something.

Suzanne just got over a bad virus and now has a cold, but she is now back to work and feeling a little better. She sent you a letter Monday so it should get there just before this one.

Tom is all right but seems to be pretty tired or is it something else? He's been doing pretty good, been working on his shack in the back and I suppose with warmer weather coming we'll be able to do more outside.

Do you need anything? Let us know if there is, and we'll ship it right off to you. I think being where you are now that more stuff is available to you. I'll write again soon. Take care.

Love Dad

While hearing from home was always welcomed, I felt differently about this letter. The tone seemed to be less optimistic and needier. My Dad was struggling at home, and this letter indicated that. I was looking forward to getting home soon because I knew how tough the early spring could be. Our long driveway would get muddy and spongy as the deep winter frost began to thaw. The old Ford tractor was down again, and Dad needed my help at home. We talked about upgrading our snow removal equipment and doing maintenance on the road before I was drafted. Apparently, the situation had deteriorated while I'd been away. The dirt road was washed out with very little stone or aggregate on the surface. When the spring thaw came, it turned the road into mud, and cars would routinely get stuck up to the hubcaps. My Dad or I would fire up the old Ford and usually be able to pull them out. There was one spot particularly prone to this muddy condition, and we planned to dump a few loads of Item 4 gravel there; but Uncle Sam got to me first, and this never happened. I needed to get home.

The other letters were from my sister and Aunt Pauline; they were easier for me to read. I tried to focus on the good things happening to them and not on my perceived notion of my Dad needing me to help him out.

I was back in full combat gear, my faded fatigues, bloused pant legs, dirty, scuffed jungle boots. I stuffed my rucksack with anything and everything I had lying around my hootch area. I gave away the 3 cans of beer I had in my fridge and a fan; taking a last look around, I made my way over to B Company area where I would revert to being a grunt.

I was restless all night, couldn't sleep thinking of where I was going, wondering how bad things were up on Linda and when I would get my orders to leave. These thoughts raced through my mind all night and sleep was non-existent. I did sleep however, as I woke startled, where was I? Oh, here back at B Company. My usual routine had changed abruptly; I was going back to war sometime today. I had to get up and get my shit together, the call could come anytime, I'd better be ready.

I made my way to the mess hall; the coffee tasted good, I always loved Army coffee, it was strong and tasty. The other stuff was just fill, the powered eggs, the hard biscuits, the chewy bacon, all edible but not very memorable. There were a few guys I knew there, we talked a bit. I never mentioned I was going back out, I knew they didn't care.

I checked in with Don and he told me he didn't know of any plans to take me out to Linda, he would holler when he found out something.

"Go draw your ammo and clean your weapon, the Armory Sgt. will be expecting you," Don instructed.

"Wada you want?" the lifer sergeant mumbled.

"I need some 16 ammo, mags and some bandoleers," I replied.

"For what?" he questioned.

"I'm going out to Linda today and I need my stuff," I shot back curtly. "I need to see the weapon you will give me and make sure it's clean." I was in no mood for his attitude.

"Okay," he grunted and provided everything I needed.

He even gave me a few banana mags, (30 round magazines) which were really not Army issue, but we all had them.

"Here sign this, and print your full name and service number below your signature, oh, you can't take the 16 out of here, but check it over," he instructed.

I looked everything over carefully, it felt good to have a weapon again; I had missed the sense of security the M-16 always gave me. The weapon looked good, a newer 16 I thought, I would clean it good when I got to Linda. I signed out the ammo and other stuff, and left. I immediately went back to the barracks and loaded the ammo into the bandoleers and tucked everything in my ammo box. My mind was spinning, I had to get focused, and I had to be ready.

As I waited to hear from Don, I decided to write some letters. My letters home never had news of where I was or where I was going; I didn't want my Dad to worry needlessly. I always tried to answer his letters and address his questions. I left the day-to-day bullshit out, and today would not be an exception to that rule. I was in a war zone; the war was still on and I was a grunt. That was the fact of the matter, nothing had changed. I was just hoping to avoid going back out to the bush, so much for hope.

"Hey Freeborn," the screen door slammed, "your chopper will be on the LZ in 30, get your shit together and get down there," Don instructed.

"How about my orders?" I shouted back, "when do I find out my DEROS date?" I continued.

237

"How the hell do I know? You're going out to the bush, maybe when you come back in," he replied.

"When is that going to be?" I pressed. He shrugged and walked out.

Great, I thought as I pulled everything together. I had to stop by the armory; it was on the way. I continued down the narrow path from the armory to the LZ and recalled my first time going out to the bush. I was more experienced now; I had seen a lot of shit, and I was no way a newbie. I was short though, and had done my job, but I still felt sick to my stomach. The adrenaline was now rushing through my body, my pace quickened, I tried extra hard to focus..."bird in bound," someone shouted, oh shit, here I go.

The flight out to Linda took about 20 minutes. I could see the hill from a distance once airborne. It was a small mountain, providing vital mortar and canon cover for the Da Nang Air Base about 20 clicks away. Our mission there was to provide security for these guns and the perimeter around the hill. I was assigned a bunker with 2 other guys from D Company. I didn't know them, but we were all part of the same Battalion. Somehow, that made me feel a little more comfortable. We were all in the same shit, and in Nam, it don't mean nothin'.

The next few days were boring and thank God, uneventful. My nights were very long and sleep came difficult, like out in the bush. I would wake often, usually startled. Noise was a problem, flairs, munitions, canon fire, mortar tube noise. It went on every night. I often thought they were just screwing around, but never sure. War can be noisy, especially on a fire base; out in the bush however the silence could be deafening, I preferred that.

It was almost a week now, and I had settled into a routine. I thought less about leaving and more about living. I had to readjust my head, get my shit together and accept this assignment, as I always did. I inquired about how long I would be out here and was told they were waiting for C Company to relieve D Company.

"Where would I be going?" I asked the platoon sergeant.

"Don't know," that's all he said.

"Home I hope," I mumbled to myself.

It was now early April; I remember thinking what an April fool's joke they played on me. The only thing was, it wasn't a joke; it was real. The firebase clerk came over near my bunker,

"I'm looking for Freeborn, has anyone seen him?"

"Here I am," I shouted back.

"I've got your orders, looks like you're going home you lucky f--k, here." He handed me the single sheet of paper with about 30 names on it.

I searched through the names and there I was. I was almost in a state of disbelief, but by having these orders I knew it was real. I checked the date and my DEROS was 15 Apr 72. I was going home. Once you have the orders, they couldn't do too much to you anymore. It was like being paroled from prison. The commanding officers had to comply and deliver me to my next duty station on the other side of Da Nang.

This war was over for me, I would soon be state side back to the world. This news took time to sink in, and finally, as I sat in the dark, musty, sand bag covered bunker, it hit me; when? When was I leaving this shit hole I wondered? I was still far away from the Company area; I had lots of paperwork to complete and travel vouchers and much more. I had to get back in, the sooner the better. I'll find out tomorrow I told myself, and spent some time praying, as I often did in Nam.

I resolved to get myself off this hill, and the next day they told me I would leave in a day or two, you'll go back in on the next regularly scheduled resupply day. I also knew I wouldn't be going back out to the bush. I wouldn't have the chance to say goodbye to my brothers in my squad. Don't mean nothin', I tried to convince myself.

Chapter 19

"Bird-in-bound," someone shouted. I looked up and there it was; the long-awaited chopper back to the rear. The chopper had mail and other stuff for the guys on Linda. I would hitch a ride back. It was my time to leave this shit hole of a country and get back to the "World".

After the chopper was off-loaded, I threw my rucksack up onto the chopper floor and jumped in, as I had done many times before. This would be my last flight over hostile territory. I instinctively clicked the safety off my M-16 as usual; I checked to see if the weapon was on full automatic, it was. This was no joy ride, Charlie still wanted to ruin my day, and that wasn't happening.

As we gained altitude and the chopper sped up, I remained on guard. I looked intently on the ground below, small arms fire were always a threat to ascending helicopters; the door gunner was also focused on the ground below. As we continued to gain altitude, I relaxed. I could see the peasant rice growers tending to their crops; I saw a few water buffalo laden down with baskets filled with rice. This was all ending now, I thought, as the chopper made its way through the heavy humid air.

The LZ was visible, a sight for sore eyes; I had made it back. I had a lot to do, but my first stop would be the Company Clerk's office, I had paperwork to complete. I was very excited and almost forgot to turn in my 16 and munitions, which was always the first stop.

"Hey Freeborn, where ya been?" Don teased. "I see you're off the hill and you probably wanna go home."

"Fuck'in A," I exclaimed, "right after I take a long shower and wash the shit off of me."

I was dirty; my clothes were stained and soiled. The Firebase was a dirty, dusty place; there was always oil and kerosene exposure. The chopper ride back was also dusty, and I hadn't showered in a few days.

"Okay," Don shot back, "but I need you to fill out these forms and issue your in-country orders," he continued.

"I'll be back," I exclaimed. I made my way to the barracks, were I found a few "stragglers", guys in the rear for one reason or another.

"Hey, where can I get some soap and a towel?" I inquired.

Someone sat up and said "in that locker," pointing to a row of unlocked wall lockers.

The locker had towels, soap and shampoo, everything I needed. I spent a good 20 minutes just letting the warm clean water wash over me, cleansing me from all the shit of the last 8 months. I was going home, my prayers had been answered, Jesus had kept his promise. Everything would be all right, just like He told me months before.

I was toweling off when Don came in the barracks, "you forgot something Freeborn," he said kiddingly.

"What?" I replied.

"Clothes, what were you planning on doing, walking around bare assed?" he continued.

I was in such a hurry I forgot to pick up a clean issue of clothes from supply. I laughed and thanked him; he was a cool guy, and I really appreciated his concern. He knew I had been through a lot these last few days, being short and all. There was always this underlying sense of consideration for guys who were short and going home. I sensed this out in the bush when guys were leaving. There were no big goodbyes, and most of the time the short timers would just leave, without a word, but there was usually that little extra consideration. Today, it was my day.

I was on cloud nine; I rushed around getting things together; I had to draw a summer uniform, everything, shoes, socks, underwear, and a dress green uniform. I had to attach the ribbons and metals I had earned on my khaki uniform; the CIB (Combat Infantry Badge) was my favorite, along with the infantry blue rope which hung off my right shoulder. Everything had to be perfectly positioned. I was now a combat veteran; all would see where I served. In Nam this was important stuff. When I returned home however, it was a different story.

The bus ride to the replacement center just outside Da Nang Air Base took about 20 minutes. I had my duffel bag stuffed with everything I was able take home. My poncho liner shirt which I bought from a Vietnamese merchant, my worn, torn jungle boots, my boonie hat, my pictures and all my letters. Everything I owned was in that bag; I would keep a close eye on it.

The replacement company was busy, lots of guys leaving and some being reassigned in-country. I was leaving because a large group of newbies had been rotated in over the past 3 months. They were our replacements; the war was still on, for them at least. For me, my time in hell was ending. I threw my duffel bag up on the bunk, looked around and thought; tomorrow I would board a bus to the "Freedom Bird".

After chow and before lights out, we talked about our adventures here in the Nam. We talked about our friends, living and dead, and even the ones we weren't sure about. Sometimes a guy would be taken out of the bush and we would never see him again. Don't mean nothin', we'd say. Now, however, it seemed meaningful as we remembered them.

These were thoughts that haunted me for months after I returned home; where are they? Did they need me? Do they resent me for leaving? Are they alive or dead? I would struggle with these questions, yes, it meant something.

I tossed and turned as I lie there on the top bunk only a few inches from the ceiling, trying to drift off to sleep. I was so cranked up; all I could do was think of home.

Before I settled in for the night I had taken off my shoes and summer uniform, and put on a well-worn pair of fatigue pants, and a tee shirt, no socks. I usually slept half dressed, a habit from my bush days. It seemed to be the most comfortable and easiest way, just in case of an emergency. We always had to be ready to move out. Now, being in this "safe" place, I still didn't feel comfortable being undressed. My uniform was neatly hanging off the end of my bunk; I placed my shoes on the floor. My duffel bag was on my bunk between me and the wall. The only thing missing was my M-16. Something always seemed to be missing when I didn't have it. It was a grunt thing.

Suddenly, a loud siren sounded, a warning of incoming mortar fire. At first it startled me, then immediately I went into combat mode. I instinctively felt around for my weapon, it wasn't there. I rolled off the bunk, put on my shoes and headed for the door. I followed the other guys to a large open top bunker. It had walls about 2 feet thick, built from sandbags. The sound of the concussion from the mortar fire was strange. As grunts, we never got mortared out in the bush; we were there trying to prevent such attacks on Da Nang. The attack lasted a few minutes, and after some time they announced all clear; we were instructed to return to the barracks. Needless to say I wasn't going to close my eyes for the rest of the night. I laid there listening, wondering and zzzzzzzzzzzzzz.

I woke to the sounds of laughter, hustle and bustle, and guys getting ready to move out. I had dosed off and didn't even realize it. I would often claim I slept with one eye open. Of course that was never the case, but I had trained myself to be a very light sleeper. In the bush, the snap of a twig would wake me, and often did.

I immediately got ready for the long flight home. We would soon board buses to the airfield, and then on to a commercial jet "Freedom Bird" for home.

After chow the buses were waiting for us. We grabbed our gear and loaded them into the belly of the buses. These were not military (cattle car) buses, but civilian buses used by the transportation contractor charged with our safe departure from Nam. There were a few MPs around, but once on the bus I did not see any signs of security. As the buses pulled out of the replacement center, I thought this is too good to be true. It was over; this long Vietnam nightmare was in my rearview mirror. Suddenly "splat" a piece of rotten melon came flying through my partially open window, spraying me with sticky, smelly juice. As I wiped the stuff off my face, I recall thinking how appropriate for this hell hole. I risked my life for these people and this is how they thanked me. It enraged me momentarily; I wanted to respond to those kids throwing stuff at the passing buses. If I had my 16, I thought; then settled down remembering I was going home.

It took what seemed to be an eternity, but I finally boarded the Boeing 707. It had spacious seating and regular commercial flight attendants. The plane had both civilian and military personnel and all the seats were filled. The flight seemed endless; we finally landed in Guam for refueling and could get off to stretch our legs. During the one hour stop over, they confined us to a holding area.

Most of the remaining flight was over the Pacific Ocean and the day was bright with nice clear views. I tried to sleep, but there was way too much noise and the excitement level was off the wall. I finally did get some z's when the day grew dark. I guess it was nighttime. Crossing the International Date Line you never knew if it was night or morning. On the horizon there was always a little sunlight, like dusk and dawn.

The early morning landing in Oakland International Airport was a welcomed event. I was exhausted from being in the air for about 23 hours. I made my way down the stairway to the tarmac and boarded one of the buses waiting for us. We got dropped off in front of U.S. Customs, and after several hours of waiting on lines, baggage shake downs, paperwork, etc., we got back on the buses for the short ride to the U.S. Army Replacement Center in the heart of downtown Oakland, California.

"Welcome Home" the large sign read, as I walked down the ramp into a large expansive room with counters and windows along the perimeter. There were barriers set up and lines formed in front of the windows. I got on one line, and again waited a long time, until finally I reached a young Army officer.

"Name," the officer said, without looking up.

"Freeborn, Joseph A," I shot back.

"What's your service number?" he continued, and I told him.

The process was lengthy; I had to answer a lot of questions, answers the young officer already knew, but he questioned me anyway. After a while the Q and A session ended, and he explained the "Early Phasedown Release Program" to me.

"You mean I can get out of the Army today?" I questioned.

"Yeah, all you need to do is sign this form waiving your G.I. Bill of Rights, and agree to serve a 6 year National Guard hitch, requiring you to attend monthly Guard meetings near your hometown, and a week each summer to play war games, any questions?"

"Where do I sign?" I replied. I immediately knew this was my way out.

I could go home and not have to go to Fort Riley, Kansas. I could reunite with my family and friends. This decision was easy for me as I never wanted to be in the service in the first place. The young officer put together a hastily prepared DD-214, my official separation papers. I was out.

"Here's your packet. It contains copies of all the documents you signed. Here's your DD-214, keep it in a safe place, it's very important," he instructed.

I got my dog tags back, my mustering out pay, money the government gives you for back pay and unused leave and a little readjustment money. It totaled $600, issued in $100 denomination traveler's checks. Wow, I was rich; I hadn't thought about money in some time. Finally he gave me my one-way travel voucher to JFK Airport;

"You'll shuttle over to Oakland Airport in a little while, your flight leaves at 1745 hours. There is a reception area in the rear of this building, wait there, they will call you. Good luck soldier."

Once in the reception area I changed into my dress greens, I was still technically in the Army. The uniform I was wearing was the summer khakis and not appropriate for early spring on the east coast.

The dress green uniform was neatly tucked in my duffel bag and made the trip nicely. I had to remove all the bling (ribbons) I was wearing on my khakis and transfer them onto my greens. It didn't take too long; I had only been in the service for 13-1/2 months. After dressing I carefully put the traveler's checks in my inside breast pocket, checking them frequently before I left Oakland.

On the plane to JFK I was surrounded by civilians from all walks of life. Some people looked at me curiously while most didn't seem to notice me at all. The flight attendants were cordial, and no one seemed too impressed with this young returning Vietnam veteran. I felt strange and out of place. I didn't even feel comfortable in the clothes I was wearing. I sat down and settled in for the 5 hour non-stop flight to JFK.

The flight home gave me time to reflect on everything that happened. I was out of the Army; I was out of Nam and going back to an unfamiliar lifestyle. The life I once lived seemed strange and distant. I had changed, my easy going, happy-go-lucky, not a care in the world persona, was gone. This war had changed my outlook on things, cynical, suspicious, cautious, guarded, might better describe the person I now was. How would I be received by my family, my girlfriend, my co-workers, my friends, I wondered? Would they see the changes in me? I didn't know, and if the truth be known, I didn't care.

The End!

A History Lesson

In writing this book I did extensive research and found very little historical accounts of the 1st/46th – 196th Light Infantry Brigade, the unit I served within Vietnam. This unit, in my opinion, was an after-thought of the U.S. commanders, keeping the war going until Nixon and Kissinger figured out a way of ending the war.

We had POWs being held in Hanoi, North Vietnam and their lives were in jeopardy during my time in Vietnam. The official term that Nixon used was "peace with honor". They had to get the North Vietnamese to the negotiating table in Paris. So, we served, fought and died in that effort. The war was unwinnable, and everyone knew it, except us. In the end, there was no peace with honor. After untold billions of dollars and 58,479 American treasures lost, where was the peace, where was the honor?

The men and women who served should have been welcomed home. There were no public celebrations or commemorative salutes to the returning young men and women. Instead, we came home literally one at a time, and quietly snuck back into our towns and cities, unnoticed, most people didn't even know we were gone.

The America we came home to had changed. The returning Vets were accused of being the dregs of society, the losers, and the poor, minorities, exploited by this unjust war. I personally was none of those, but yet major political figures still contend that's what we were. They believed the cream of the crop had escaped being drafted or had influential friends that kept them out of harm's way. Nothing could be further from the truth. We were from all socio-economic groups. We had top performers from high schools throughout the U.S. We had West Point graduates; we had the best this country produced.

When I got home in 1972, the protesters were in charge, the veterans were shamed for their service. Speaking from my own experience, I can honestly say I felt no gratitude from anyone. When we needed America the most, America was embroiled in corruption, guilt and civil unrest. The America we returned to was in crisis.

Many veterans came home to broken relationships, divisions among family members and little or no economic support. To illustrate this point, I read a "conspiracy theory" that our government and major employers conspired against the returning Vietnam veterans by developing a "black list". This list was derived from the veterans' DD-214 (separation document). The DD-214 contained embedded codes which indicated our behavior, our sexual preferences, our drug use, and many other details all negative, and all unsubstantiated. This is denied by the government, but plays into my own experience and many other returning veterans who couldn't get jobs or housing or any support. We were on our own.

The Vietnam vets earned their commendations after the war. They came home, brushed themselves off and went about living their lives. Each and every one of us had to struggle and overcome the effects of Vietnam. Most were able to put this war aside, and others were not. Heroes all, nevertheless.

I record the following Vietnam history lesson for future generations, my grandchildren and all Vietnam Veteran's families. The war in Vietnam is no longer studied in schools here in the U.S. Many of the teachers and professors today were protesters against the war in the 60's and 70's. There were many actors and entertainers who also demonstrated against the war, and in my opinion contributed to the loss of many men and women in Vietnam. They actually believed they were helping to end the war, but in fact they prolonged the conflict by tying our hands behind our backs.

If America fails to learn from the mistakes of this war, then America is sure to repeat them.

The following account is based on the article "The Vietnam War: Why It Was Impossible for the U.S. to Stay Uninvolved," by Colonel William Wilson, U.S. Army (ret.), in the April 1997 issue of Vietnam magazine, which granted permission for portions to be excerpted in this book.

NOTE: I italicize my comments which are not part of the original article.

In January 1961 when John F. Kennedy was elected the 35th President of the United States, he claimed "the torch had been passed to a new generation". He also challenged the American people to "Ask not what your country can do for you, but what you can do for your country". These words were met with great excitement and hope for a better post World War II future.

Immediately upon taking the Office of the President, Kennedy was faced with a deteriorating situation in South East Asia, South Vietnam. At the time most people had never heard of Vietnam, so the news was greatly ignored.

A general in Laos, another far off distant country, Major General Phoumi Nosavan, an American friend, was a prominent political figure and border line dictator. He was born in Savannakhet, the French Protectorate of Laos, in January 1920. Originally he served in the French colonial administration as a low level civil servant.

257

Then joined the resistance movement against the Japanese occupiers, late during WWII.

Nosavan as a military leader in Laos, he left much to be desired, losing several battles in the early 1960's, and now losing ground to a pro-Communist group supported by the Soviet Union (Russia). Rioting Buddhists and students were tearing South Vietnamese cities apart. Murder squads were dispatched killing South Vietnam officials and some early U.S. Military Advisors. The Army of the Republic of South Vietnam (ARVN) fought half-heartedly against the insurgent Viet Cong causing U.S. concern.

In August and October 1963 the U.S. gave its support to a cabal of South Vietnamese generals who were planning to remove Diem from power. Diem rise to power had been the anchor of American Vietnam policy for nine years. President Kennedy had been kept informed every step of the way, through CIA agencies. The CIA had an operative Lieut. Col. Lucien 'LuLu' Conein in Vietnam. An eccentric yet professional agent, Conein had contacts in Vietnam.

Conein was born in Paris, France and raised in Kansas by his aunt. He kept his French citizenship and enlisted in the French Army at the beginning of WWII. He deserted a year later when France surrendered to Germany. The U.S. Office of Strategic Services (OSS) recruited him to parachute into France with a French resistance unit. After the War in Europe ended, Conein joined a company of French and Vietnamese commandos to harass Japanese posts in northern Vietnam. He entered Hanoi, North Vietnam in 1945 working with the OSS team.

In Violation of the Geneva Accords, Conein assumed the cover role of an advisor to the Saigon Ministry of the Interior, a deception that allowed him to garner intelligence on conspiracies against the government. His job was delicate; since he had to be sure that his reports of the upcoming coup were not only to Diem but American sympathizers within the regime.

These facts as reported in the Pentagon Papers, also stated Washington did not originate the anti-Diem coup; nor did America intervene to prevent the assassination of Diem and his brother Ngo Dihn Nhu, Diem's chief advisor. For weeks the American mission maintained contact with the plotting generals through Conein.

U.S. Ambassador Henry Cabot Lodge Jr. described Conein as an 'indispensible man' who was friends with General Tan Van Don, figurehead commander of the South Vietnamese army for 18 years. The general had confidence in Conein and was reluctant to deal with anyone else.

The Pentagon Papers cited a cablegram dated October 5, 1963, from Ambassador Lodge to the U.S. State Department describing a meeting between Conein and General Doung Van Minh. General Minh who was very popular with his ARVN troops (who nicknamed him 'Big Minh'.). Minh was chosen to be the leader against Diem. Conein did not respect Big Minh, and referred to him as a 'glorified French Army corporal' However, Minh had stated Conein was the only American he could trust. Big Minh did not expect any American support, but needed assurances that the U.S. would not interfere with his plans. He also needed assurance that the U.S. would continue to provide military and economic support. He had to act quickly, as there were numerous plots to overthrow Diem.

The subsequent messages from the White House indicated the National Security Council would support a coup that had 'a good chance of succeeding'. They also stressed that they would offer no 'active promotion of a coup,' and the desire for 'plausible denial'. After one coup attempt failed, the White House told Lodge to discourage the plot if quick success seemed unlikely. Lodge replied that the United States was unable to 'delay' or discourage a coup.

On August 29, Lodge sent a cable to Washington, demanding decisive measures. He stated, **"We are launched on a course from which there is no turning back because U.S. prestige is already publicly committed to this end in large measure, and will become more so as the facts leak out. In a more fundamental sense, there is no turning back because there is no possibility, in my view, that the war can be won under the Diem administration."**

President Kennedy's approval gave Ambassador Lodge complete discretion over U.S. aid to Diem. Lodge now had a mandate to manage American policy in Vietnam, thus to topple the Diem regime.

In November 1963 the coup proceeded on schedule. When Diem asked Lodge about the U.S. attitude towards his regime, Lodge told him he was not well enough informed to say, but told Diem, "If I can do anything for your personal safety, please call me."

Conein, armed with his ivory-handled .357 Magnum frontier model revolver, was summoned to a rendezvous spot, carrying a satchel containing 3 million piasters (Vietnam money), the equivalent to $40,000 US, in case the insurgents needed funds. He was equipped with two telephones, one linked to the main CIA office and the other to his villa, where a team of American Special Forces personnel was guarding his family. Conein also had a radio in his Jeep so he could transmit prearranged cipher that signaled the start of the coup.

The South Vietnamese generals telephoned Diem and promised to allow him and his brother Nhu to leave the country unharmed, if they capitulated. At first he refused, then realizing he could no longer hold out, he and his brother slipped into a Land Rover and drove to Cholon, the Chinese suburb in Saigon.

After an unsuccessful attempt to negotiate, Diem phoned Minh to say he would surrender unconditionally and that he and Nhu were in Saint Francis Xavier, a French Catholic Church in Cholon. An M-113 armored personnel carrier and four Jeeps under Minh's bodyguard commander, Captain Nhung, were sent to the church. As they left the church, Big Minh signaled Nhung by raising two fingers. By every account, Nhung then sprayed both brothers with bullets.

General William C. Westmoreland, who replaced General Paul Harkins as commander of MACV, summed it up this way; **'In his zeal, the young president made a grievous**

mistake in assenting to the overthrow of South Vietnamese President Ngo Dihn Diem in 1963. In my view that action morally locked us in Vietnam. If it had not been for our involvement in the overthrow of President Diem, we could have perhaps have gracefully withdrawn our support when South Vietnam's lack of unity and lack of leadership became apparent.'

On a personal note, I was in 7th grade when all these events were happening, I remember some of the details at the time, but I never knew the U.S. had such an influence on the instability of that far off 3rd world country. The war was heating up, or was it? Was President Kennedy going to back away from this situation, and perhaps live to fight the Communists another day? We will never know. I believe that day of November 22, 1963, sealed my fate, and thus, this story. As the author of this book, and having lived this story, I am sure of one thing. When we were called into service to our country, we came ready to serve. We did not doubt our government, nor did we ever consider running away from this call to service. It is the defining attribute of the American patriot, and all the men and women who gave their all, to the service of our country. The Vietnam Veteran.

In Memory of a Life Well Lived

Dan Gerleve passed away at the age of 64, in 2016. I dedicate the writing of this book to him and what he meant to me while in Vietnam, and long after we returned home. Dan and I were the first to connect after Nam, sometime in the early 80's.

Dan grew up in Hanover, Kansas with his parents and siblings. He never married and worked as a CPA for a government agency.

He never spoke about his life before Vietnam, and only mentioned his parents and siblings occasionally. Dan was a very private man and kept things to himself.

In Vietnam, Dan was a source of strength and solace for me. When things got bad, he was always there to put things in perspective. He had a huge warm grin, which seemed to say to me, all was well. He was the guy you would go to, for anything, and he would always help. Dan was a kind and gentle man, standing 6'2" with a strong farm boy build. There weren't any self-serving or self-seeking aspects about him. Here I am, take me or leave me. I am who I am. That's the message I always got from him.

The last time I saw him was in the fall of 2014, when another Nam buddy, Bob Hampel, invited me to his weekend cabin in Massachusetts. Dan was visiting Bob at the time. We spent the day reminiscing and recalling those days so long ago. Dan still looked amazingly fit and hadn't changed much over the years. For me and Bob, the same could not be said.

I miss Dan and I will never forget his kindness and gentleness in a war void of those things. He stood out among those I served with. He distinguished himself as an exemplary soldier, and friend.

Glossary of Terms

AK-47 –Automatic Russian made Kalashnik AK-47 weapon used by VC.

AO – Area of operation.

ARVN – Army of the Republic of South Vietnam.

Assistant Pig Gunner – A man designated to assist the pig-gunner, (M-60 Machine Gunner) providing cover and feeding the weapon with ammunition.

Bandolier – A cloth type apron which stores magazines of ammunition.

Birds-in-Bound – A term used to announce helicopters were landing.

Bloused – A term used to describe the wrapping of pant legs around the soldier's leg to prevent insects and other undesirable things from crawling up the leg.

Booby-trap – An explosive device used by the enemy to prevent U.S. troops from accomplishing their mission.

Bouncing Betty – Also known as the German S-mine, (Splintermine in German). When triggered, these mines would launch in the air about 3 feet and detonate, projecting a lethal spray of shrapnel in all directions.

BTOC – Battalion Tactical Operation Center.

Bush – The jungle, mountains, rice paddies, basically all areas soldiers patrolled looking for enemy activity.

C-130 Aircraft – Troop and cargo transport airplane used in Vietnam.

C-4 – Plastic explosive

Cache – A collection of items in a hidden or inaccessible place.

Cellulitis – A skin rash or rough skin which was usually itchy. Also known as "jungle rot".

Glossary of Terms

Chinook Helicopter CH-47 – A large double propeller helicopter used to transport troops and lift heavy objects. also called "Shit-hook".

Charlie – The military phonetic word for the letter C, also a nickname for the Viet Cong.

Charlie Four – The phonetic term for C-4 plastic explosive.

Chop-Chop – Hurry up.

Clacker – A small hand held firing device used to detonate a Claymore mine.

Claymore Mine – An explosive device consisting of a pound of C-4, metal plates of steel balls, encased in a heavy plastic housing. This device was used for perimeter security.

Click – One kilometer.

Cluster Fuck – A term used when troops got too close together. Also referred to phonetically as "Charlie-Foxtrot".

CO – Commanding Officer.

CP – Command Post or Position.

C-rats – C-rations, food in cans for field consumption.

CS – Tear gas

DEROS – Date Expected to Return from Overseas.

DI – Drill Instructor during basic training.

Dinks – A derogatory term used in Vietnam referring to the VC.

DMZ – De-militarized Zone, the defined area between North and South Vietnam.

DP – A guard position out in the bush.

Glossary of Terms

D-Ring – A special device used to clip on equipment, enabling easy access to items such as canteens, ammo, etc.

Drop – A reduction in DEROS time. An early out in Vietnam.

Early Phasedown Release Program – A program offered to some returning Vietnam vets giving them a chance to get out of the service before their required time.

EM Club – Enlisted men's bar/restaurant.

Freedom Bird – Any plane returning to the USA (civilian or military).

Grunt – Combat soldier in Vietnam.

Gunships – The cobra AH-1H helicopter equipped with rockets, 40 mm cannons and mini-guns.

Hard Five – Sergeant E-5 three stripes differentiating it from a Specialist E-5.

HHC – Headquarters and Headquarters Company.

Hootch – Name used to describe military or civilian housing in Vietnam.

Hot – An area or region under enemy fire.

Hump or Humped – Meaning to move on the ground, usually with full pack.

JFK Airport – John F. Kennedy International Airport, Queens, NY.

KIA – Killed in Action

Kit Carson Scout – ARVN soldiers working with U.S. troops.

LIB – Abbreviation for Light Infantry Brigade.

LRPP – Long Range Patrol Packets, freeze dried food.

LZ – Landing Zone

LT – What we called our lieutenants in Nam.

Glossary of Terms

M-16 – A gas-operated, air cooled automatic/semi-automatic assault weapon weighing 7.6 pounds with a 20-round magazine. Maximum range 2,350 meters. Maximum effective range 460 meters. Automatic firing rate 650-700 rounds per minute, sustained automatic firing rate of 100-200 rounds per minute.

M-60 – The standard American light machine gun. A gas-operated, air-cooled, belt fed automatic weapon. Often referred to as "The Gun" or "The Pig".

M-79 – An American single shot 40 mm grenade launcher, called the Thumper.

M-203 – A single-shot 40 mm grenade launcher, mounted under the barrel of the M-16 assault weapon. (It was classified during the Vietnam War).

MACV – Military Assistance Command Vietnam.

Magazine – A metal housing designed to hold 20-30 rounds of M-16 ammunition. Aka as Mags.

Monsoon Season – Rainy season in Vietnam, October through February.

MP – Military Police.

NCO – Non-Commissioned Officer.

NDP – Nighttime defensive position where troops would rest at night.

Newbies – Troops in-country less than 1 month.

Night Hawk Huey Gunships – See Gunships.

Panzies or Panzie – Nick name for John DeSantis, owner of a Gulf gas station and a good friend of the authors.

Point Man – A person designated to lead a squad, usually involving cutting through thick growth and canopy.

Glossary of Terms

Pound Cake – A canned c-rat delicacy usually enjoyed with canned peaches.

PZ – Pick-up Zone.

R&R – Rest & Relaxation – a two-week leave during a tour of duty.

REMP – Rear Echelon Military Personnel – non-combat soldier.

RO - Radio operator.

Sapper – Enemy demolition–assault team.

Shake n' Bake – An 8 week training program for draftees during the Vietnam War. These draftees would lead other draftees' at the most basic level.

Shinola – A brand of shoe polish, used in an expression "you don't know shit from Shinola"

Slack Man – A person who walks directly behind the point man, providing an extra set of eyes and ears for him.

Slicks – Nickname for a Huey Helicopter.

Starlight Scope – A special sighting device, allowing the operator to see in the dark.

Stand-down – A term used when a unit would be removed from service during a conflict or war. It was also a term used when troops were returned from the bush and allowed to rest.

Sqdn. - Abbreviation for Squadron.

Squad – 9 or 10 men with various responsibilities, led by a sergeant within a platoon.

Tan Son Nhut – Major U.S. airbase in Siagon, South Vietnam.

TOP – Company First Sergeant.

Glossary of Terms

Trip wire –A thin, almost invisible wire connected to an explosive or warning device.

TT – A term used in Nam to mean in a hurry, soon or quickly.

UH-1H – Official designation of the Huey Helicopter.

Vietnamization – U.S. policy to withdraw troops, transferring responsibility and direction of the war effort to the Government of South Vietnam,

Vills – A grunt term for Villages.

VC – Viet Cong- Gorilla fighters.

Web seating – Slings of web belting used as seats on C-130 aircraft.

World – Home in the USA.

Zippo – A name brand of a cigarette lighter widely used in Vietnam.

CPSIA information can be obtained
at www.ICGtesting.com
Printed in the USA
LVHW032113011222
734346LV00003B/414